Art in Saudi Arabia

Hot Topics in the Art World

Published in association with Sotheby's Institute of Art

Series Editors

Jeffrey Boloten and Juliet Hacking, Sotheby's Institute of Art, London

This series of short, thought-provoking and sometimes controversial books debates key issues of current relevance to art-world professionals working in both the private and public sectors. The texts give wider visibility to some critical areas of professional art-world practice, considering what disruptors are challenging the status quo and how the art world is likely to be transformed over the next decades as a result.

International Series Advisory Board

Art in Saudi Arabia

A New Creative Economy?

Rebecca Anne Proctor with Alia Al-Senussi

LUND HUMPHRIES

Sotheby's INSTITUTE OF ART

First published in 2023 by Lund Humphries
in association with Sotheby's Institute of Art

Lund Humphries
Huckletree Shoreditch
Alphabeta Building
18 Finsbury Square
London EC2A 1AH
UK
www.lundhumphries.com

ISBN (hardback): 978-1-84822-639-5
ISBN (eBook PDF): 978-1-84822-649-4
ISBN (eBook ePub): 978-1-84822-648-7

A Cataloguing-in-Publication record for this book is available from the British Library

Designed by Crow Books
Set in Caslon Pro and Sofia Pro
Printed in Estonia

Contents

Foreword

With global crude oil prices continually volatile, the Saudi government has crafted a policy of economic diversification that will see a gradual reduction in its dependence on oil exports and a steady expansion of other revenue-generating sectors. One of the most high-profile of these projects is the fostering of a new creative economy in the Kingdom. As public funding for the arts in Western nations continues to dwindle, in Saudi Arabia unprecedented resources are being invested into cultural infrastructure. Whereas spectacular museum-building, arts events and the acquisition and display of Western masterpieces are a distinguishing feature of other Gulf State soft-power initiatives, uniquely the art that is being pushed to the fore of the Saudi cultural agenda is by resident or diasporic artists.

In this illuminating and thought-provoking book, the authors – both deeply connected to the Saudi art world and its global reach – clearly and systematically confront such questions as: 'Is it possible for an autocratic regime deploying a top-down approach to foster a genuine creative economy and cultural infrastructure?' and 'are today's artists free to express themselves?'. The authors also bring to light the little-known history of art culture in the Kingdom, analyze what is at stake in the current Saudi Renaissance, and examine the question of whether such intensive investment will successfully serve to promote grass-roots art production and the home-grown Saudi art world.

Jeffrey Boloten and Juliet Hacking, August 2023

Acknowledgments

We would like to thank those who have offered insight in relation to the text, as well as numerous Saudi artists, individuals and creative practitioners who have entrusted us with their personal stories regarding art creation during this moment of great cultural, social and economic change in the Kingdom of Saudi Arabia. Special thanks to Saudi artist and writer Abdulrahman Al-Soliman who graciously has assisted us with fact checking art-historical events, Basia Kearey, Martha Wakeman, Robert E. Proctor, Katrina Kufer, Wejdan Reda and Antonia Carver.

Introduction

Art as a Catalyst for Social Change in Saudi Arabia

An art scene has long existed in the Kingdom of Saudi Arabia. Since 2016, when Crown Prince and Prime Minister Mohammed bin Salman, more commonly known as MBS, launched the Kingdom's Vision 2030 reform agenda, the country's cultural scene has come into the spotlight and been subject to development at breakneck speed. Top-down investment in the Kingdom's cultural sphere is being undertaken in tandem with MBS's socioeconomic reforms, with the goal of ushering in an era of social and economic transformation to diversify Saudi Arabia's economy away from oil.

This book will describe the thriving contemporary Saudi art scene and how an art scene has long existed in the Kingdom and has been influenced not only by the history and economics of the Saudi state, especially the discovery of oil and changing role of traditional Islam, but also by geopolitics. A major theme will be freedom of artistic expression and the place of art in Saudi society and education within the context of centralized and recent massive government patronage.

At the heart of Saudi Arabia's social change is Vision 2030. The reform plan intends to transform the Gulf nation into a modern and vibrant society; diversify Saudi Arabia's economy away from oil; and develop a robust public service sector. Among the priorities of Vision 2030 is culture.[1] Through the encouragement of creativity, particularly among Saudi youth – the largest segment of the Kingdom's population (in 2020 children and young people represented 67 per cent of the Kingdom's total population) – the Saudi state hopes to foster innovation in all sectors of the economy, to think creatively through a massive state-wide program implementing exposure to art and culture. MBS's reform agenda encourages the population, especially the young, to think in ways that lead to entrepreneurship and business models as sources of non-oil income. MBS has also opened the once closed country to foreign visitors. In September 2019 Saudi Arabia launched a tourist visa scheme to welcome international visitors and increase tourism to the Kingdom.

Approximately half of Saudi Arabia's gross domestic product is generated from the oil and gas sector, which accounts for nearly 70 per cent of its export earnings. Of concern to the Kingdom is the volatility of oil prices and revenues, which remain uncertain. Saudi Arabia has therefore realized the urgency of diversifying its economy. It is betting on culture as a means to do so. Other fields the Kingdom is investing in in order to diversify include strategic investments through the Public Investment Fund (PIF), Saudi Arabia's sovereign wealth fund, mining, industrial zones, manufacturing, technology, green energy, tourism and sports. It has so far been successful. Between 2000 and 2019, the Gulf Cooperation Council countries (except Bahrain) are among the top 20 nations to have improved Economic Diversification (EDI) scores over that period.[2]

During a panel discussion at Expo 2020 Dubai, held in 2022 after being postponed due to the COVID-19 pandemic, Albara Al-Auhali, Deputy Minister of Cultural Strategies and Policies at Saudi Arabia's National Identity Enhancement Program supporting Riyadh's new transitional JAX District neighborhood (discussed in detail in Chapter 2), described Saudi's growing arts hubs around the country as ways to foster 'job opportunities that help grow and diversify the economy'.[3] Amr AlMadani, Chief Executive Officer of The Royal Commission for AlUla (RCU) (discussed in Chapter 2), told the World Economic

Forum in 2021 that the Kingdom's plan for investing in the arts will contribute up to 3 per cent of its total GDP by 2030, generating US$20 billion in revenue and creating over 100,000 jobs by the year 2030.[4] This will include the building of more tourism infrastructure, improved access to the UNESCO-designated historical city of AlUla, and 'statement architecture' – such as is being done through Riyadh Art, a civic initiative under the auspices of The Royal Commission for Riyadh City (RCRC), also part of Vision 2030, that will transform public spaces in Riyadh, where specially commissioned public artworks will highlight creative expression, beautify the city and accelerate the development of Saudi Arabia's cultural economy.

The money is there to push for change. In 2022 Saudi Arabia's economy grew at its fastest pace in a decade due to booming oil prices and increasing output, with its GDP rising by 9.6 per cent year-on-year in the first quarter, according to Bloomberg.[5] While governments around the world are cutting investment in art and culture, notably in the United Kingdom and the United States, Saudi Arabia is investing unprecedented levels of wealth into culture. At the end of 2021, for example, Saudi Arabia announced a US$64 billion investment in its entertainment sector. The Kingdom's increased ability to spend is due partly to oil prices bouncing back after the COVID-19 pandemic and surging towards US$100 per barrel, but elsewhere the increase in the non-oil economy can be attributed to the push the Kingdom has made over the last few years towards the establishment of a creative economy.

What is a creative economy? The term has become a new buzzword in the contemporary socioeconomic lexicon. According to John Howkins, who popularized the term in 2001, 'creative economy' is based on people's use of their creative imagination to increase an idea's value. Howkins used the concept to describe economic systems where value is based on novel imaginative qualities rather than on traditional resources of land, labor and capital.[6] The term is used to describe creativity through an entire economy rather than just creative industries. Some, such as the United Nations Conference on Trade and Development (UNCTAD), which has worked to shape the global understanding of the creative economy since

2004, believe that creativity is the defining characteristic of developed 21st-century economies.[7] The United Nations describes creative economy as having 'no single definition. It is an evolving concept which builds on the interplay between human creativity and ideas and intellectual property, knowledge and technology. Essentially it is the knowledge-based economic activities upon which the "creative industries" are based.'[8]

External commentators note the psychological impact of the rapid social and cultural changes as Saudi Arabia pursues the creation of its creative economy. As Bernard Haykel, Professor of Near Eastern Studies and Director of The Institute for Transregional Studies at Princeton University, argues,

> Cultural change in Saudi Arabia has taken the form of shock therapy and it is a complicated phenomenon. There is something like a cultural war taking place within Saudi Arabia between the forces of reaction and those at the top, along with many young men and women, who wish the society to change. The effort is to make Saudi Arabia be different from what it was in the past in a variety of ways. It is not just about rock concerts and art exhibitions.[9]

Over the last decade, beginning with the reign of King Abdullah and implemented most radically since 2015 when MBS came to power, change has come to the Kingdom of Saudi Arabia. Many Saudi creatives have now returned from abroad, and those who stayed are able to create their art with fewer restrictions, now encouraged by the Saudi state as well as a host of new private art entities founded by Saudi nationals and by foreigners (see Chapter 5). The many cultural events, in the form of film festivals, art exhibitions and music concerts, that are now present across the country are testament to Saudi Arabia's repeal of its more conservative policies. There are now large public concerts and cinemas – both of which had been banned since 1979 – which have been operating in cities across the nation since 2018. Throughout the year, festivities dedicated to music, film, art and, as of January 2022, even yoga have sprung up at various cities in the Kingdom.

As Kristin Smith Diwan, Senior Resident Scholar at the Arab Gulf States Institute in Washington, says, it seems as if 'the authority of the religious police has now been replaced by the General Entertainment Authority [established in 2016], and one could add the Ministry of Culture, which is now playing a leading role in supporting the creative industries'. She adds: 'The appetite for a cultural change in Saudi Arabia was evident even before the start of King Salman's reign. One could see it in the irreverent art salons, YouTube skit comedy collectives, and emergent filmmakers. But a full opening could not be achieved without a shift in the government's posture.'[10]

That shift, when it came, was dramatic. Most Saudis will describe the rate of change as astonishing. Prince Khalid bin Bandar bin Sultan bin Abdulaziz Al Saud, the Saudi ambassador to the United Kingdom, noted in an October 2021 interview with *The Times*, '1,000 laws have been altered or removed over the past five years. Particularly impressive is the progress of women's rights. Since 2018, women can drive, travel abroad, marry and divorce without their male guardians' permission. Public places of gathering are now co-ed.'[11] These freedoms have, however, emerged at the same time as several disturbing cases in which the Saudi state has either been directly or indirectly involved. These include the confinement of social activists; maltreatment of migrant workers; the 2017 imprisoning of members of the Saudi elite at the Ritz-Carlton in Riyadh allegedly to crack down on corruption; and the killing of the Saudi journalist Jamal Khashoggi at the Saudi Consulate in Istanbul in 2018.

These events shocked and perplexed. The nation's critics continue to question whether social and cultural change in the Kingdom is but a propagandistic attempt to divert attention from human rights violations. Saudi Arabia's effervescent and growing art scene, with its fervent support from the state, continues despite international skepticism, boycotts from international cultural organizations and even the global press itself.

In 2021 the Ministry of Culture reported that the Kingdom hosted 100 cultural events, led by 25 new cultural organizations established by the Ministry of Culture. These events include two biennials produced by the Diriyah Biennale Foundation: The Diriyah Contemporary Art Biennale, which held its first edition in December 2021, and the world's first Islamic Arts Biennale, which opened in January 2023. The Contemporary Art Biennale (see Chapter 2) featured a rich roster of local and international artists. It was curated by Philip Tinari, Director and Chief Executive of UCCA Center for Contemporary Art in Beijing, on a scale previously unseen in the Kingdom. 'We are privileged to witness a moment of dynamism, optimism and openness, and with it, transformative change', Tinari said in his opening speech.[12]

Saudi Arabia's cultural revolution has often been construed as 'artwashing' by its critics, who argue that the promotion of art and artists is intended to distract from or legitimize misdeeds by individuals, organizations or the government. But Saudi artists, curators, gallerists and supporters reject the term 'artwashing' (discussed more in Chapter 4). Saudi artists will tell you that the Saudi art scene is not a place for propaganda. They are not told what to create nor what message their work should convey. 'I am not part of some propaganda machine', stated Saudi artist Muhannad Shono, selected in 2022 to represent the Kingdom at the 59th Venice Biennale, about the controversial first showing of Desert X AlUla in January 2020.[13]

The art and culture now being shown and exhibited to local and international visitors at present events and exhibitions, and planned mega and giga projects, is like nothing ever seen before in the Kingdom. It has the potential to initiate a meaningful cultural dialogue between Saudi Arabia and the rest of the world. And yet observers from afar may still question how a country can develop a robust art and cultural scene within a political structure that doesn't adhere to the Western ideals of liberal democracy. Although it is common currency in the West that countries need a liberal democracy to have a free and vibrant creative scene, Tinari argues that this is not always the case: 'There was a time when we looked at art and forward-thinking, cultural expression happening in non-democratic places as a prelude to a teleological political change towards a democratic system, but meaningful cultural production and meaningful urban culture is happening in contexts that are not elective democracies."[14]

In writing this book, documenting recent contemporary Saudi art history has been challenging. The dearth of scholarship that records this history makes facts difficult to come by. We have tried to present the most factual portrayal possible, relying in part on the experience of both of us in working over the past decade in the Kingdom. We realize this book offers just an introduction to the rapidly expanding and fascinating Saudi art scene. We take responsibility for whatever inaccuracies there may be in our account of the recent and heretofore under-researched history of Saudi art. We hope that this book assists local and international audiences to better understand the shifting face of art and culture in Saudi Arabia during a time of great change.

1

From Past to Present: The Sources of Saudi Arabia's Culture Drive

The history of art in Saudi Arabia reflects the country's wider sociopolitical and historical realities. Where one might find a linear progression of an art scene that gathers strength, moving from early pioneers to dynamic rising stars and popular awareness, as has been the case in the art scenes of Europe, North America, Latin America and parts of Asia, the trajectory of art in the Kingdom of Saudi Arabia has been different. It mirrors the jolts of the Gulf nation's geopolitics and economics that are tied to its oil wealth and rentier-state mentality, going from openness and growing popular acceptance to closure and isolation followed by a dynamic burst of movement at breakneck speed.

The Effects of Oil and Religious Politics on Artistic Growth

On 3 March 1938 oil was first discovered in Dhahran, a city in Saudi Arabia's Eastern Province. On that day, when Standard Oil of California drilled its well, thereafter known as 'Prosperity Well', it unlocked the biggest source of petroleum in the world and changed Saudi Arabia forever. Saudi artist and former physician Ahmed Mater's 2010 lightbox *Evolution of Man* captures how the relentless quest for oil has affected the changing fate of Saudi Arabia. It depicts a silhouetted gas pump that mutates into a human x-ray, with a gun to its head, before it moves back into the gas pipe – a foreboding artwork capturing the destructive and cataclysmic nature of Saudi Arabia's oil wealth ever since its founding. 'I am a doctor and confront life and death every day, and I am a countryman at the same time', said Mater in 2010. 'I am the son of this strange, scary oil civilization . . . our lives changed completely. For me, it is a drastic change that I experience every day.'[1]

The Kingdom is presently the world's biggest annual exporter of petroleum. It possesses 17 per cent of the world's proven petroleum reserves.[2] When oil was discovered, Saudi Arabia was a young country, having only recently been formed on 23 September 1932, when by royal decree the two kingdoms of the Hejaz (a region in the west of the country) and Najd or Nejd, which forms the geographic center of Saudi Arabia where Riyadh is located today, were unified under the name of the Kingdom of Saudi Arabia. The consolidation of these kingdoms was the work of Ibn Saud or Abdulaziz bin Abdul Rahman Al Saud, the first King of Saudi Arabia (1932–53). It was a period shaped by strident regional debates on identity-making – influenced largely by Ibn Saud's victory and his support for Islamic revivalists that would greatly bolster pan-Islamism and nationalism across the Islamic world.

From the late 1930s, as foreigners – predominantly Americans – arrived in Saudi Arabia, lured by the big business of oil, so too arrived the cement for the construction of new edifices, and lots of fast shiny cars, shopping malls and, increasingly, a consumerist culture. All of this took place within a moderate practice of Wahhabism – the term used to describe the Kingdom's dominant faith according to the reform doctrines of the 18th-century Arabian Islamic scholar Muhammad ibn Abd al-Wahhab (1703–1792), practiced in the Kingdom as its official form of Islam and major creed.

The discovery of oil, and the money that came from it, led to great changes in Saudi society – changes that impacted education and the teaching of art. Following the Second World War, when new artistic movements such as Abstract Expressionism and Conceptual art were developing internationally, young promising artists in Saudi Arabia were participating in the birth of their very first non-traditional artistic movement led by foreign art teachers arriving in the country. The blossoming of an artistic community coincided with the country's transition from a Bedouin nomadic culture to an urbanized modern society after the discovery of oil and establishment of the nation.

During the 1950s a Western education system was introduced to the Kingdom and with it came the study of art at school. It brought in teachers, including those for studio art, from Egypt, Lebanon, Syria and Palestine. By 1951 there were over 200 schools across the Kingdom.[3] The first approved curriculum for art education in elementary, intermediate and secondary educational grades was established in the latter part of the decade and implemented as an essential part of Saudi Arabia's education system.[4] Art education was known as 'arts and crafts' and its aim was to train young boys and girls in manual skills as well as to teach them perseverance and self-confidence.[5] The introduction of art classes inspired the showing of art publicly, leading to the first public group exhibitions in the Kingdom, staged at the time by the Ministry of Education in Riyadh.[6] Due to the lack of dedicated art spaces, artists would often show their work in schools. Promising art students began being sent abroad to other Arab countries or to the West to further their art education.[7] These included Mecca-born Saudi sculptor and painter Abdulhalim Radwi (1939–2006), considered the pioneer of modern Saudi art and known for his vibrant abstract canvases. He and his contemporary Dia Aziz Dia (b.1952) were among the first to be sent abroad on a government scholarship to study at the Accademia di Belle Arti in Rome. Radwi received his degree from the Accademia in 1964 and Aziz Dia received his in 1971.[8] Aziz Dia's encounter there with Surrealism inspired his portraits of the human face and figure. Upon his return, he produced key public works, including the relief on the Saudi Airlines building in Jeddah, as well as a sculpture at the entrance to Mecca.[9]

Then came the oil boom of the 1960s, and Saudi Arabia, enjoying its wealth as global demand for oil increased, engaged with the world. In 1960 the Organization of the Petroleum Exporting Countries

(OPEC) was founded in Baghdad, Iraq, with the signing of an agreement in September 1960 by five countries: Iraq, Kuwait, Saudi Arabia, Venezuela and the Islamic Republic of Iran. Their goal was to control their countries' most precious resource: oil. For much of the 1960s through to the oil crisis of 1973, as the global demand for oil increased, the Kingdom witnessed a period of growing artistic productivity and openness to the world, supported at a state level. This period witnessed the continuation of generous art scholarships by the government, enabling a growing creative class to study abroad in the world's greatest cultural capitals.

The Saudi government also sponsored an increasing number of female artists to pursue their studies abroad. Among them was Safeya Binzagr (b.1940), one of the Kingdom's foremost artistic pioneers. She studied in Cairo and is known for her Social Realist and emotive canvases reflecting social and traditional life in the Kingdom's Hijaz region. For many, Binzagr's portrayals of Saudi individuals are surprising given the influence of conservative Islam, which while moderate at the time, was present. Binzagr is one of the only Saudi artists who painted the human form and displayed her work publicly prior to 1979. She was from a prominent merchant family in Jeddah, noted one Saudi artist on condition of anonymity, which afforded her more social freedoms at the time. In 2000, Binzagr, dubbed to this day the 'mother of Saudi art', opened her own museum and gallery in Jeddah called Darat Safeya Binzagr, where several artists also trained. Filwa Nazer (b.1972), a contemporary Saudi artist now based in Jeddah who works in a variety of media focusing on questions of emotional identity in relation to social and spatial contexts, studied drawing and painting in oil, pastel and watercolor, as well as taking life-drawing classes at Binzagr's center from 2001 to 2003. Binzagr's contemporary Mounira Mosly (1954–2019), on the other hand, who also was sent on a state-funded scholarship to study art in Cairo, is known for vibrant abstract paintings and mixed-media artworks largely exploring political issues in the Arab world, particularly the Palestinian struggle and the impact of regional wars on children.

The mid-1960s saw a flurry of artistic activity, including a 1965 solo exhibition for Radwi in Jeddah, considered to be among Saudi Arabia's first official art exhibitions, and the establishment of the Institute for Art Education in Riyadh, one of the first of several government-funded institutions of the mid-1960s dedicated to building a robust domestic arts education system.[10] More triumphs came for notable male and female Saudi artists during the late 1960s, largely from state-led initiatives and funding. In 1968, Radwi founded the Fine Arts Center in Jeddah with government support, where he served as Director until 1974. He later became Director-General of Culture and Arts for the city from 1980 to 1992. Women artists were increasingly paving their own way in the growing Saudi art scene. In 1968, at the Dar Al-Tarbia Al-Hadetha school in Jeddah, Binzagr and Mosly became the first Saudi women to show their work publicly in the Kingdom. In 1973 Mosly became the first female artist to hold a solo exhibition in the country's capital of Riyadh.

Despite strong government patronage for the arts, the first art exhibitions in Saudi Arabia were often not well-attended.[11] Public disapproval of the visual arts may have reflected the Kingdom's conservative Islamic practices that did not allow depictions of human figures or living forms – a rule meant to distinguish Islam from polytheism and the use of icons and representations of Jesus in Catholic Christianity. While the Quran does not ban images of living beings, the practice of discouraging image-makers is attributed to the authentic hadiths – which Muslims believe to be a record of the words and actions of the Prophet Mohammed as transmitted through narrators across centuries. According to the hadith of Ibn Abbas, one of the Prophet's cousins, 'Every maker of graven images will be in Hellfire'. It should be noted, however, that restrictions can be found in all monotheistic religions. Judaism, Islam and Protestant Christianity follow to the letter the prohibition of 'graven images' set in the Ten Commandments in the Book of Deuteronomy, the fifth book of the Old Testament.[12] Drawing human or living species was strictly forbidden and monitored in Saudi Arabia after 1979, in accordance with a strict abidance to Wahhabi Islam, and continued to be discouraged until around 2016.

Despite the restrictions of conservative Islam and the public's uncertainty over displays of visual art in public, the 1960s and 1970s witnessed the first examples of state patronage in Saudi Arabia as well as the birth of social art institutions. The growing scene of Saudi artists, whose careers had flowered thanks to government support, garnered local and international awareness. They also enjoyed a stimulating intellectual and creative exchange with artists elsewhere in the Gulf, across the Arab world and beyond, which in turn encouraged more state patronage.

Saudi Arts Patronage as State-Building Exercise

A high point, and one that fervently expresses the growing passion for local and international art of the time as well as the increasing role of the Saudi government in the arts, took place during the early 1970s when Mohamed Said Farsi (1936–2019), who was Mayor of Jeddah from 1972 to 1986, commissioned numerous public sculptures for the port city on the Red Sea. Noted as the first mayor to introduce Western art to a major Arab city, Farsi commissioned sculptures by eminent international and regional artists of the period, including Henry Moore, Joan Miró, Victor Vasarely and Jean Arp, Lebanese artists Aref El Rayess and Shafiq Mazloum, and Egyptians Mustafa Senbel and Salah Abdulkarim.

According to Farsi, art was a necessary part of a thriving urban environment, and so he set to beautify Jeddah. He funded his project with money from public donations and his own. In just over a decade, Farsi created an open-air museum in Jeddah featuring over 400 sculptures. Yet over time many of them were damaged. Today just 20 line the Jeddah corniche, the sunlight of the Red Sea glistening through their abstract shapes.[13] The sculptures depict traditional Saudi items including coffee pots, incense burners, palm trees and abstracted parts of camel bodies to avoid the portrayal of a full living creature, in accordance with Islamic belief of the time.

Farsi's unprecedented investment in the visual arts attracted the attention of local and international media, leading many to view Jeddah as the Kingdom's city for art and culture while Riyadh was the seat for the royal family. His artistic patronage also caught the attention of the Saudi state. During the 1970s, awash in unprecedented revenue from oil, the state increased public spending for art and culture. In 1974, the unmatched budget of US$630 million (around US$3 billion in today's value) for the beautification of Jeddah, part of the city's five-year development plan, demonstrated the Saudi state's increasing patronage of art.[14] It was Farsi's opinion that the people of Jeddah would have greater regard for their city if functional public works could be balanced by works of art exemplifying grace and dignity.[15]

In addition to his urbanization project for Jeddah, Farsi also engaged with local artists by personally supporting arts programs and exhibitions in the city. His artistic passion fueled his state-building enterprise through culture and encouraged other artistic events in Jeddah. During the 1970s, art exhibitions were sponsored by and held at foreign embassies in Jeddah, with ambassadors and senior members of foreign missions in attendance – a testament to the growing openness and support of foreign missions to the development of art in Saudi Arabia.[16]

During this period Faisal bin Abdulaziz Al Saud served as King from November 1964 until his death in 1975. A time beset by growing geopolitical and economic tensions, including two Arab-Israeli wars and the oil crisis of 1973, it was also a time of modernization and reform. King Faisal's foreign policy was characterized by pan-Islamism, anti-communism and pro-Palestinianism. He also tried to limit the power of Islamic religious officials. In many ways King Faisal was a revolutionary for Saudi Arabia, introducing television and public education to the Kingdom, and even outlawing slavery in 1962. He also led the oil embargo of 1973, announcing a boycott of the Kingdom's oil sales to the United States because of President Nixon's military support for Israel in the October War against Egypt and Syria. The ensuing Arab oil boycott caused the price of oil on the world market to multiply nearly five times, prompting a global financial crisis but profiting the Kingdom.[17]

King Faisal's policies witnessed an increase in art patronage, exhibitions and artistic communities. For example, during the 1970s, new social institutions became central to the development of the cultural scene in Saudi Arabia. One was the Saudi Arabian Society for Culture and Arts (SASCA), a civil society institution headquartered in Riyadh and founded in 1973 to encourage young artists and to promote the arts locally and internationally.[18] Such institutions provided much needed means of support for artists to continue to make their work.

However, despite the growth of the Kingdom's art scene, uncertainty clouded the visual arts sector. Patrons reduced their involvement as geopolitical and economic tensions rose during the late 1970s, leading to increased Islamic conservatism and hence opposition to the visual arts.[19]

Artists such as Ahmed Mater emphasize that it wasn't until the end of the 1970s that the beginning of a 'sustainable, independent infrastructure for the arts' in the Kingdom came into being.[20] This was also a period in which Saudi Arabia experienced the most social and political instability since its founding, which included, in 1975, the assassination of King Faisal nearly 11 years after he had deposed his brother, King Saud.

While King Faisal's reign was largely popular among Saudis, his secular reforms were frowned upon by conservatives, leading to violent protests. In 1966 Prince Khalid, the King's brother, led an attack on a television station and was shot dead by a policeman.[21] King Faisal managed to successfully stabilize the Kingdom's bureaucracy until his assassination by his nephew, Faisal bin Musaid, in 1975, after which he was succeeded by his half-brother, Khalid (1975–82). One theory attributes King Faisal's assassination to the secular reforms that he introduced, as well as the tensions between Saudi Arabia's practice of conservative Islam and the need to maintain its role as the birthplace of Islam, alongside the increasing consumerism of the country resulting from oil wealth and foreign influence.

A 2013 altered black-and-white photograph by Saudi artist Abdullah Al-Jahdhami, who goes by the name of Shaweesh, in many ways illustrates the surreal nature of Saudi Arabia's struggle with modernization. It shows Faisal, then a prince and foreign minister, signing the Charter of the United Nations in San Francisco in 1945, next to Yoda, a Jedi master from the *Star Wars* movies known for his unusual style of speaking and small size. Shaweesh told the BBC that he included Yoda in the picture because both Yoda and Faisal were 'wise, strong and always calm'.[22] In 2017 the image accidentally ended up printed in a Saudi school textbook. A senior education official was fired for the mistake. Shaweesh's rendition of the iconic image of King Faisal is also an example of how Saudi artists have explored the struggles of their own history through art within an often conceptual and kitsch style where messages are hidden and not outrightly relayed (see Chapter 4).

In 1979, right before a period of cataclysmic change, Saudi artist Mohammed Al Saleem (1939–1997), who was also one of the few Saudi artists to have studied abroad on a government scholarship, at the Accademia di Belle Arti in Florence, founded Dar Al Funoon Al Sa'udiyyah (The Saudi Art House). It was a place that hosted Saudis and non-Saudis, and provided students and emerging artists with free art supplies.

Yet tensions continued to afflict Saudi society, and the spell of growing attention to the arts waned. The Kingdom, wealthy from oil and entangled in geopolitics, grappled with its conservative religious forces, which despite the country's relative openness and practice of moderate Islam during the 1970s, still propelled it towards a sudden period of rupture, a turning point that would thrust the country into a state of isolation. The extreme wealth from oil and its threatening influence on the Kingdom's ultra-conservative religious society was like a pressure cooker waiting to burst.

The Year of No Return: Artistic Effects of 1979 and its Aftermath

In the early hours of 20 November 1979, as around 50,000 faithful Muslims gathered for prayer in the courtyard surrounding the Kaaba in Mecca, Islam's holiest place, a charismatic 40-year-old fanatical

Muslim preacher by the name of Juhayman al-Utaybi led a group of four to five hundred men inside. They mingled with the worshipers. After the imam finished prayers, Juhayman and his followers pushed him aside, seized the microphone and proclaimed that the Mahdi, or 'redeemer of Islam', the divinely guided one that Muslims believe will come at the end of time to rid the world of evil and injustice, was arriving. Juhayman announced that the ruling Al Saud dynasty had lost its legitimacy because it was corrupt, ostentatious and had destroyed Saudi culture by an aggressive policy of Westernization. He instructed his men located near the shrine's gates to take up sniper positions within its tall doors, which overlooked the city of Mecca. Worshipers were shocked to see the sight of armed gunmen in a space where the Quran strictly prohibits violence. A few gunshots were fired, and in just one hour, Juhayman and his men took over the Grand Mosque or Masjid al-Haram, the holiest mosque in Islam. Juhayman called for the overthrow of the House of Saud and a return to the original ways of Islam, a repudiation of the West, the expulsion of non-Muslims from Saudi Arabia and the abolition of television. It was a radical reaction to the Kingdom's increasing consumerism and Westernization that had resulted from oil wealth.

For two weeks, until 4 December 1979, Juhayman and his followers occupied Islam's House of God while Saudi forces fought to reclaim the Masjid al-Haram. Hundreds of militants and worshipers were killed in the crossfire as the Grand Mosque's seizure shocked the Islamic world. Juhayman and 67 of his fellow rebels who survived the assault were captured and beheaded by the Saudi government.

The sociopolitical effects of Juhayman's revolution on the Kingdom of Saudi Arabia sent radical new shockwaves through a country that was only just beginning to modernize and open up to the world. As a result of this lethal mixing of violence and religion, the Kingdom, to protect itself from the recurrence of such horrifying events, closed to the outside world and entered a period of extreme Islamic rule, plunging into total isolation. 'When oil came, we became a rich state and through this wealth our traditions were being influenced; we were forced to change and adapt. How do you stop change?' asks Maha Al-Senan, Saudi art historian and advisor to the Ministry of Culture, of the 'change' that Juhayman wanted to put an end to. 'You use religion to justify it and politics as a tool', she adds. 'What ensued in Saudi Arabia after 1979 was largely what Juhayman wanted.'[23]

A few months earlier, and just a few hours away by air from Mecca, another Islamic revolution was underway in Iran led a by radical Shia cleric by the name of Ruhollah Khomeini, and one which many scholars say inspired Juhayman and his followers. Iran's Islamic Revolution was also linked to the treasure and trouble of the country's oil wealth and the rising expectations of the Iranian people after the 1973 increase in the price of oil. Faced with mounting economic difficulties and sociopolitical repression by the Shah's regime, the revolution, led by Khomeini, overthrew the monarchical government of the ruling Pahlavi dynasty leading to the theocratic government of Ayatollah Khomeini and the present-day Islamic Republic of Iran, which continues to govern the country through its harsh Islamist Shi'ism.

These religious upheavals had a profound effect on the way art was created in both Saudi Arabia and Iran. 1979 was a turning point for the Middle East. The twin revolutions, as they are often described, within the region's two biggest powers have pitted Iran and Saudi Arabia against each other ever since, and resulted in similar social constraints for both Iranians and Saudis, impacting how they go about their everyday lives. While this book focuses on the Saudi art scene, it is crucial to underline how the sociopolitical and economic events of the period had everlasting effects on the creation of art in the Kingdom. For Saudi society at large, the geopolitical events inside and outside the Kingdom during 1979 were harbingers of things to come. The Iranian Revolution sparked the world's second oil shock in five years, triggered by a drop in oil production in its wake, and led to a drastic increase in the price of oil, resulting in fuel shortages worldwide similar to those of the earlier 1973 oil crisis. Other events that took place that same fateful year of 1979 – among the most important and tumultuous in modern Middle Eastern history – included the invasion of the Soviet Union into Afghanistan;

the signing of the Camp David Accords between Israel and Egypt; and the launch of General Zia ul-Haq's Islamization program in Pakistan. These concurrent events took place during the Cold War and the battle for influence between the United States and the Soviet Union. All of them rocked the world and the region, transforming the Middle East's geopolitical and social landscape into what it is today.

A growing conservative Islamic air had swept the Kingdom in the months prior to Juhayman's seizure of the Grand Mosque. It took the form of resistance to a growing presence of foreigners, particularly foreign women, which led members of the clergy to curb practices deemed offensive to Islamic principles. At the top of the list were unsuitably dressed foreign women shopping or eating out. Religious leaders wanted to protect Saudi society from the ways of Westerners. The new conservatism seemed to strike a chord in the Kingdom: Saudi women who had never had to cover their faces began to don the niqab (a black veil covering the entire face except for the eyes) and wear black gloves and thick stockings.

The harshness of this period was witnessed by art students. Halla bint Khalid (b.1971), an artist based in Riyadh who attended a private school for girls during the 1970s and 1980s, recalls how as a schoolgirl she was told to eliminate images of human beings and animals. 'In primary school, upon receiving our textbooks at the start of the year, we were ordered to get out our rulers and draw a line across the neck of every breathing image in the book', she says. 'It was as if we were killing them, I remember feeling extremely uncomfortable, even frightened, but I knew that disobedience meant humiliation and possibly severe punishment. I was also confused, if these textbooks were distributed by our government, how come they had "haram" [meaning 'bad' in Arabic] images in them?! Who gave these orders? Our school, or another authority?'. Art classes were held but students were strictly forbidden from drawing 'anything with a spirit', as bint Khalid puts it. 'We were to stick to depicting landscapes that we could not see and still lives. I remember painting a kitten and unsuccessfully trying to hide it from the teacher. To my surprise, she didn't tear it up or report me, she simply nodded, and gave it back silently indicating that I should put it away.'[24]

Manal AlDowayan, known for her poignant and edgy portrayals of Saudi women and the challenges they face, says the changes to the way her art teachers told her to represent living beings came in phases. She grew up in the Eastern province on the Saudi Aramco compound in Dhahran and distinctly remembers her experience while attending public schools. 'In 1979, when I entered first grade, I was still drawing normally', she recalls. 'From second, third and fourth grade the rules for how we were allowed to draw kept changing. First it was: "draw whatever you want," then it was "draw a line over the neck of any living being" and then it was "don't draw anything that was human, just draw sunsets or the desert or nature or a still life."'[25]

After 1979, the nascent arts, theater, cinema and music that characterized much of the 1960s and 1970s in Saudi Arabia gradually dwindled as an increasing ambiance of Islamic conservatism prevailed. The curtain came down on a growing era of arts and entertainment, and the government closed all the cinemas and theaters; the separation of sexes in public spaces ensued, as did the control of women by their male guardians, among other harsh rules, as a political response to curb an increase in Islamic activism. The new tightly controlled and segregated environment made it very challenging for artists to have exhibitions in the Kingdom. Both male and female artists living in Jeddah at the time describe a gradual change in the way they were expected to dress, live and socialize. Many more stringent religious edicts followed.

In a desire to counteract the effects of Western consumerism and thwart further revolution, Saudi society had gone into reverse. After 1979, travel to Saudi Arabia was by invitation only, and largely for male businessmen. With rare exceptions, no unmarried foreign woman under the age of 40 was allowed in the Kingdom. During these years of ultra-conservative rule, the art scene did not vanish completely, but it was naturally forced underground. Still, some initiatives, like artist Mohammed Al Saleem's Dar Al Funoon, which was inaugurated in 1980 by Prince Fahd bin Fahad Al Saud, continued staging shows and enabling artists to gather and meet until it closed in 1995 due to lack of funding. Islamic conservatism was not the only reason that government support for arts and culture dwindled during the 1990s, argues Al-Senan. 'The economy took a huge hit during the Gulf War; there was no money to sponsor art, exhibitions or collectors who wanted to buy art', she says.[26]

Writing defiantly in 1976 as if he foresaw the changing circumstances for art creation post-1979, Al Saleem passionately expressed his belief in the survival of art and creativity in the Kingdom despite the growing conservatism of the present period. 'Many may be misled on the subject of culture, describing it as backward, or falling behind the parade of civilizational progress. That is wrong, for culture, by its very nature, is continually evolving as long as there is a natural continuation of life.'[27] During the 1980s and 1990s, non-traditional art forms were suppressed by conservatives, who used their social and religious influence to challenge the modern and contemporary practices they opposed. Most types of art, except traditional Islamic art disciplines such as poetry, were repudiated and banned from the educational system for being inconsistent with the tenets of Islam and the hadith.

There is little documentation on art creation in the Kingdom during the 1980s and 1990s. Loring Danforth, in his article 'Art Evolution: Saudi Arabia', calls the period the most 'extremely conservative' in the Kingdom's history.[28] He also reflects on how official political reaction to the tense environment of the 1970s was responsible for driving the arts underground. Danforth notes that:

> religiously based restrictions on the mixing of men and women; on photography and the depiction of the human form; and on women's freedom of dress, movement, and employment were strictly enforced . . . It was difficult for the few Saudi artists working in the country to obtain the materials they needed. They had to purchase paint and canvases from abroad; they even found it difficult to buy art books, since depictions of the human figure were forbidden. Female artists couldn't attend the openings of exhibitions of their own work.[29]

Life had changed for an entire generation of Saudis who lived through the 1980s and 1990s period of uncompromising social and religious conservatism. The geopolitical situation of Saudi Arabia and the wider Middle East led Saudi artists at home and abroad to explore issues of identity, as male and female Arabs growing up in a strictly conservative socio-religious society struggled to find their sense of self and place both domestically and abroad. 'Art is parallel to life and my creative journey is reflective of the bigger context of what happened and is happening in Saudi Arabia', explained Jeddah-based artist Filwa Nazer, who returned to the Kingdom permanently in 2018 after six years of living in London. 'I am from that generation, and I grew up in a very conservative Saudi Arabia and that had a direct influence on my early work, which explores themes of escapism in relation to extreme religious and social restrictions', said Nazer. 'As a teenager I wanted to break free in so many ways. Television was quite limited and reading became my escape; it widened my horizons and helped shape my thinking. At the time I was driven by curiosity of other cultures and in search of beauty elsewhere.' The generation to which Nazer belongs witnessed extreme religious conservatism in parallel with economic prosperity brought on by the oil boom. 'How do we look back and reflect on the psychological and sociological impact?' she asks. 'We come from Islamic Arab countries. Tradition and religion always existed, conservatism to some extent existed, but post-1979 it took a different shape and religion became political.'[30]

During this time of fundamental Islam, an entire generation was denied the cultural education that had nurtured the creativity of the early pioneers. Moreover, during the 1980s and 1990s, fundamentalist movements such as the Sahwa (an Islamic ideology calling for an end to Western cultural influence, which had been developed during the 1950s and 1960s by Muslim Brotherhood members fleeing persecution in Egypt) rose to prominence in Saudi Arabia. It was another trend that frustrated artistic creativity. Because of the scarcity of materials, restrictions on freedom and limited support from the government, only Saudi artists who worked underground or studied abroad continued to produce art.

Throughout the 1980s and 1990s, conflicts raged within and outside of the Kingdom's borders. Artists were influenced by the highly mediatized geopolitical narratives of the time that were relayed to the public largely through satellite television and newspapers. After the 1978 coup in Afghanistan installed an unpopular communist government, Saudi Arabia, along with the United States, became the main financer of the mujahideen – militant Islamic fighters in the Soviet-Afghan War. Saudi political consciousness was overtaken by the huge influx of investment to train the anti-Russian Islamic militants. Art education and cultural events were sidelined. The dominant mode of thought was how to bolster a national and religious agenda to support the mujahideen.

There were a few artistic gems during the period. One was the Al-Mansouria Foundation, set up in 1999 by Her Royal Highness Princess Jawaher bint Majed bint Abdulaziz to support creativity in Saudi Arabia and nurture local artists. The other was Al Muftaha Art Village, founded in 1989 in Abha, the capital of the Asir region in the southern part of the Kingdom, by Prince Khalid Al-Faisal bin Abdul Aziz Al Saud, Governor of Asir region from 1971 to 2007. The village became an inspiration to aspiring artists living in Abha, including Ahmed Mater (b.1979), Abdulnasser Gharem (b.1973) and Ashraf Fayadh (b.1980), a Palestinian refugee born in Abha. A great lover of the arts as well as an avid painter and poet, Prince Khalid made Abha – which to this day is amongst the more conservative regions of the Kingdom – one of the creative hotspots of the era. 'Prince Khalid would come once a week to the village to open exhibitions and check on the artists working there', recalls Fayadh.[31] In 1999 Prince Khalid established Painting and Patronage, an organization meant to build bridges of cultural, artistic and educational understanding between the Arab world and the international community. He also set up the Literary Club of Abha, the Abha Singing Festival and the Abha Prize for Cultural Excellence. In 2008, when he became Governor of Makkah, he set up the Cultural Council of Makkah.

Conflicts raged like an ongoing storm that rises and falls. Just as the Soviet-Afghan conflict drew to a close at the end of the 1980s, a new conflict reared its head: the First Gulf War. It began in the summer of 1990 after Iraq invaded Kuwait. Operation Desert Storm, a 42-day military operation carried out against Iraq by an international coalition, which included Saudi Arabia, led by the United States, began on 17 January 1991.

During the same period, satellite television was introduced to the Kingdom and broke the monopoly of the religious establishment in the information space. People began seeing movies and sitcoms. 'The dry parched culture of fundamentalist Islam started to be watered and this created a fertile ground for young Saudis of the time like Mohammed bin Salman to understand and relate to the greater world', says Ali Shihabi, Saudi Arabian author and commentator on Middle Eastern politics and economics.[32] Saudi television was filled with unprecedented coverage of the Gulf Wars in the form of image-saturated propaganda used to justify the violence against the Iraqi forces. They were images that would influence Saudi artists for years to come.

The late 1990s and early 2000s saw a new flowering of artistic activity, this time firmly contemporary in nature. One big artistic gamechanger was the Internet, which was made available in Saudi Arabia in 1999. Saudi artists, most of whom were and still are self-taught, could now search the web to educate themselves on art history and the art movements taking place outside of the Kingdom – particularly relevant for those who did not travel frequently. A rise in Conceptual art among Saudi artists during these years is often attributed to the lack of art materials, restrictions on the depiction of the human form, and the highly controlled religious and politically conservative climate.

As impetus for artistic creation, platforms such as Al Muftaha Art Village and the Al-Mansouria Foundation offered a place of refuge from the harsh ambiance of the time, but there seemed to be no escaping the socio-religious and political effects of the Kingdom's years of ultra-Islamic rhetoric and rule. The events of 11 September 2001 fractured a sense of Saudi national identity, particularly due, as many artists will state, to Western media defamation of the Kingdom as a backward, fundamentalist country that brewed jihadists. For a country that had been plunged into isolation for so long, 9/11 was the latest extremist event, the result of the lethal concoction of fundamentalist religion, aversion to Western ideology and oil wealth.

Abdulnasser Gharem's 2014 work *Pause* is his personal response to 9/11 – an event where the world, as he puts it, 'paused' and which has affected much of his artistic output ever since. A former military officer in the Saudi Arabian army, Gharem's diptych comprises tiny rubber stamps in Arabic and English depicting the Twin Towers of the World Trade Center, with a plane just beginning to crash into the first, as if paused forever in time. On the left side is a golden arch with words from Sandy Dahl, wife of United Airlines Flight 93 pilot Jason Dahl, who said: 'If we learn nothing else from this tragedy, we learn that life is short and there is no time for hate.'[33]

On that fateful day, Gharem was in his hometown of Khamis Mushait, a city located to the east of Abha, the capital of the Asir region in southern Saudi Arabia, watching television with his family. When he heard the names of the Saudi hijackers, four of whom were from Khamis Mushait, he realized that two had been his classmates. It caused him to ponder what led them – both were well educated and from good families – to take such a horrific path while he became an artist. He says he asked himself 'Why wasn't it me?'. Was it the fiercely controlled Islamic society in which he and others grew up that sent them – and many others – to their demise? 'I realized I could not fall back on the culture I had grown up in. I then began to believe that all religions and ideologies based on a coercive model for the universal common good have failed and I decided to create my own path.'[34]

It seems almost serendipitous that a year after that fateful date, in Abha, there occurred the formation of the artistic movement Shatta – which means in Arabic 'to be broken up, dismantled' – at the Al Muftaha Art Village, led by self-taught artists from the Asir region: Gharem himself; Ahmed Mater, who had previously been a physician; Ashraf Fayadh; Abdulkarim Qassim; and the poet Muhammad Khidr. Just like its name, the members of this collective called for a deconstruction of modern Saudi art practice, which had its origins in Western modernism, and the creation of something new from the remnants of what had come before. 'Art in its modern style is not something that is Saudi', says art historian Maha Al-Senan. 'It is something that is imported.'[35]

2

A New Saudi Arabia: Art on the Frontlines of Social Transformation

After the events of 9/11 and the 2003 US invasion of Iraq, there was a new hostility towards Saudis from the West and, coupled with the extreme Islamic religious political ideology that was taught in schools in the Kingdom at the time, the artists who founded the artistic movement Shatta, as notes Abdulnasser Gharem, were feeling depressed and confused. 'We didn't know what to do and so we turned to art', he said. The artists of Shatta wished to establish a collective approach to art-making that could be at once collaborative, disruptive and transformative. They also wanted to examine ideas of what art could be in Saudi Arabia, and to do so in a different style to that adopted by artists in Al Muftaha Art Village, who had been taught by visiting art professors from Palestine and Sudan and emulated a Western modern approach to art creation. 'We wanted to make a break from Western modern art concepts and do something different, something new', explains Ashraf Fayadh. 'Those concepts didn't represent us culturally. We needed to develop our style that comes from the depth of our culture and our society, one that mirrored our life which is different from that lived in Europe.'[1] Shatta sought to define an art form that was entirely new, born from the context in which its artists had grown up and were living, and from the everyday materials around them. According to Ahmed Mater, by sharing their studios the artists found 'both new modes of self-expression and like-minded people. These were creative sparring partners equally preoccupied with the possibilities and shortcomings of the burgeoning cultural scene in the unlikely town of Abha.'[2] Additionally, the Internet provided the Shatta artists with a new source of knowledge and a way to communicate with the rest of the world.

In 2003, on the eve of the US invasion of Iraq, a chance encounter at the Al Muftaha Art Village between British cultural entrepreneur Stephen Stapleton, Abdulnasser Gharem and Ahmed Mater led to the founding of the artist-led cultural organization Edge of Arabia (EOA), which defines itself as being set up to 'encourage grassroots cultural dialogue in Saudi Arabia and between Saudi Arabia and the Western world'.[3] EOA became a beacon of light for the art scene in Saudi Arabia – a new way for artists to gain visibility abroad and a means of forging cross-cultural dialogue between the East and the West. 'Edge of Arabia was a pioneering idea, a new platform for showcasing Saudi Arabian artists not only at home but also abroad', said Abdullah K. AlTurki, who was EOA's Creative Director between 2007 and 2013. 'At the time there was little opportunity to see Saudi art anywhere, and suddenly Edge of Arabia offered access to it and worked towards changing perceptions about Saudi through artistic projects, exposing Saudi art in places like London, Istanbul, Venice and Berlin. It was truly groundbreaking on many levels.'[4]

EOA launched its first exhibition in London in 2008, and over the following five years introduced a new generation of Saudi artists to the world, breaking down stereotypes of the conservative Gulf nation as lacking in art and culture. Notable exhibitions and programs include its 2011 *Future of a Promise* at the Venice Biennale and the 2012 London exhibition *#cometogether*, as well as cultural diplomacy and residency projects.

Despite the conservative shroud that still lay over Saudi society, arts organizations, galleries, patrons and artists were finding ways to create and show art within a climate of restrictions. The art, in many ways, was born from the restrictions – freedom of expression was found through a conceptualist language, through signs and metaphorical symbolism (explored in Chapter 4).

New private patrons that came on the scene included the Jameel family, among the Middle East's most prominent and philanthropic art patrons. The family's tradition of social entrepreneurship and community development stems from the late Sheik Abdul Latif Jameel who founded Abdul Latif Jameel, a family-owned diversified business, in 1945. In 2003 Art Jameel was established by Fady Jameel, the grandson of Abdul Latif Jameel, as part of Community Jameel, set up to continue the Jameel family's tradition of supporting their community in Jeddah – a tradition initiated during the 1940s that now supports similar communities around the Middle East, setting up art institutions, including artist residencies, art prizes and art collecting, all of which support the growth of the region's art scene.

As one of Saudi Arabia's premier non-governmental organizations dedicated to art and culture in the Kingdom and throughout the Middle East, the vision of Art Jameel, which is funded primarily by the Jameel family (it receives no money from the Saudi state), is to document, nurture and excavate cultural histories and the contemporary realities of the Arab world. Since its launch, it has established major cultural centers in Jeddah, Cairo and Dubai.

Another crucial private player whose vision dates back to 2008 is the Saudi Aramco-sponsored King Abdulaziz Center for World Culture, or Ithra, which means 'enrichment' in Arabic, a term evocative of its vision to create a cultural institution for 'social progress through education and cross-cultural exchange'.[5] It was in 2008, on the 75th anniversary of Saudi Aramco, that King Abdulaziz announced his desire to build a center that promised a continuous journey of merging the arts, culture, science and technology to inspire creativity and also thrust Saudi Arabia into what Ithra calls a new 'knowledge economy', one whose vision reflects similar ideals to the Kingdom's current drive towards a creative economy. King Abdullah, King Abdulaziz's son, laid the framework for Ithra, and in 2016 the dream of both late kings came to life. Located in Dhahran on the site of the first commercial Saudi oilfield, and designed by Norwegian architectural firm Snøhetta, the center comprises a museum, children's museum, library, cinema, theater and numerous exhibition halls. It works with artists both from the Eastern Province and across the country, as well as internationally.

In 2013 another major private art establishment came into being: the Saudi Art Council (SAC). Led by Princess Jawaher bint Majed bin Abdulaziz and a group of art patrons in Jeddah, in 2014 SAC inaugurated the council's annual curated exhibition week, named 21,39 after the city's geographical coordinates. 'With the inception of SAC and specifically the 21,39 annual exhibition, it became possible to consistently exhibit the work of local artists in Jeddah', said Abdullah K. AlTurki, a founding member of SAC. 'What was interesting about SAC was its focus on Saudi artists and Saudi audiences. SAC was also an important entry point for international visitors like EOA was before.'[6] The organization has been an important anchor for the Kingdom's art scene ever since, alongside the establishment of Athr Gallery in Jeddah in 2009, co-founded by Mohammed Hafiz and Hamza Serafi. It was followed by Hafez Gallery, also in Jeddah, in 2014.

While Riyadh did not develop a commercial art scene during this time, nor did it have the cultural community of Jeddah, a few galleries sprung up in the Saudi capital, including Alaan Artspace, which opened in 2012. Its first exhibition, *Soft Power*, featured works by prominent Saudi female artists such as Manal AlDowayan, Sarah Abu Abdallah and Sarah Mohanna Al Abdali, whose work portrayed daily life in the Kingdom, exploring issues of identity for Saudi women.[7] Alaan Artspace closed in 2017 and its founder, Neama Al-Sudairi, opened Lakum Artspace, which functions as a multidisciplinary space for art and design, in Riyadh in December 2021.

Saudi Arabia 2.0

As the art scene continued to develop, thanks to a host of private patrons and artist-led initiatives, changes to Saudi Arabia's ruling House of

Saud ushered in a new period of immense socioeconomic change and one that used art, culture, tourism and entertainment as its driving force. When King Abdullah passed away on 23 January 2015, Salman bin Abdulaziz Al Saud became King and his son, Mohammed bin Salman (known as MBS), became Deputy Crown Prince and Minister of Defense – a role that gave him the power to pursue his audacious plans for reform: Vision 2030. His national transformation plan, meant to wean the Kingdom off its reliance on oil and move it towards the establishment of a creativity economy, thrust Saudi Arabia into fast-forward motion through a series of reforms aimed at the creation of a new Saudi Arabia – one that liberated the country from its ultra-conservative past; built a new economy separate from oil; and gave its people freedoms that had been denied to them for decades.

From the time MBS assumed his new role as Crown Prince in 2017, a series of announcements and reforms placed culture at the forefront of Saudi Arabia's future and made it part of its masterplan for social transformation. Where post-1979 art and cultural engagements were initiated by artists and private patrons, in 2017 the Saudi government took a top-down approach to transforming the nation and its relationship to the world through culture. 'Culture didn't have the attention it required in Saudi Arabia [prior to this period]', says Qaswra Hafez, the founder of Hafez Gallery in Jeddah. 'When I want to learn about a country I am traveling to, how do I learn about it? One major way is through culture. For a very long time the entire world did not know how to relate to us because we were not sharing our art and culture with them.' What we are seeing now in Saudi Arabia for art and culture, quips Hafez, is a 'U-turn with a rocket strapped on its back'.[8]

The Ministry of Culture is the key institutional player in this seismic shift. While it was established in June 2018, its origins date to 1962, when the Ministry of Information was founded to oversee information and media. It was renamed the Ministry of Culture and Information in 2003. In 2018 Prince Badr bin Abdullah bin Mohammed bin Farhan Al Saud was appointed as Saudi Arabia's first Minister of Culture. He continues to occupy the role of Governor of the Royal Commission for AlUla, a post he has held since the body was created in July 2017 to oversee archaeological and tourism projects in the governorate of AlUla, the Kingdom's ancient area spanning 200,000 years of history.

Prior to 2018 Saudi Arabia had no singular governing entity overseeing art and culture. The creation of the ministry celebrates culture as a crucial element for societal growth and change. 'Art and culture are transformative and by that we mean they have the power to change things', states Prince Badr.[9] A new era came to the fore, a Saudi 2.0 that championed the belief that creative practice through art and cultural activities could diversify the economy – rescuing it from diminishing oil resources – change society and, ultimately, preserve the regime.

A New Face for Saudi Culture

On 11 December 2021, at the opening night of the first Diriyah Biennale, the mood was euphoric, vibrant and hopeful. Approximately one thousand guests from Saudi Arabia, the foreign press, and regional and international art professionals gathered outside the newly opened and sleekly designed Diriyah Biennale Foundation in Riyadh's new JAX creative district of Diriyah. In the air was a steadfast belief that times had changed for the conservative Kingdom and that the future held much promise.

Saudi Arabia is no stranger to art exhibitions, but the Diriyah Biennale marked a new chapter for the Kingdom's art scene. Many Saudis will say that the massive social changes the Kingdom has undergone began during King Abdullah's reign (2005–15), but it wasn't until MBS became Crown Prince that they stood out for their breadth and rapidity. They have also been well publicized. From 2017 MBS touted numerous reforms to rebrand the country's image at home and abroad. These included restricting the powers of Saudi Arabia's religious police, the Mutawa, and improving women's rights. In June 2018 MBS lifted the ban on women driving. In August 2019 he loosened the male-guardianship system by allowing women over the age of 21 to obtain passports and travel abroad without permission from a male guardian, and granted them rights to register a marriage, a divorce and a birth; to obtain family documents; and to be the legal guardian of a child.

Along with these social reforms came large government expenditure on culture. The goals of this massive investment are twofold. One is to decrease the Kingdom's reliance on oil and expand the economy through creative enterprises. The other is to foster a new image for Saudi Arabia – just a few years ago considered a closed off ultra-conservative country. Now it is becoming a 'Mecca' for artists and cultural tourism.

Culture provides a means for Saudi Arabia to communicate with the outside world in a way that transcends the geopolitical complexities of its contemporary history. On 27 March 2019, during a ceremony in Riyadh, Prince Badr unveiled the Ministry of Culture's mission statement titled 'Our Culture, Our Identity'. It outlines how arts and cultural projects aim to support international exchange and cultural understanding while also contributing to Saudi Arabia's economic growth. 'The Ministry is creating opportunities for global cultural exchange, because through exchange you break down barriers and build understanding', said a spokesperson for the Ministry. They continued:

> The diverse cultures of the world will benefit from knowing each other better. Finally, culture can also contribute to the economy, and provide jobs and growth. Art and culture are transformative and by that we mean they have the power to change things. They can positively impact economies and societies by binding communities together. Art and culture can build understanding between people and provide new forms of expression. They can also help citizens understand their past and raise their aspirations for the future. In short, art and culture make people's lives better, and that is what the Ministry of Culture is all about.[10]

As part of the Kingdom's massive social and cultural transformation, new government bodies like the Ministry of Culture continue to grow and develop. In February 2020 the ministry announced the creation of 11 new bodies, including commissions for museums, visual arts, architecture, design, fashion, culinary arts, heritage and literature, among others – each with its own financial and administrative independence.[11]

The billions of dollars that Saudi Arabia is investing into art, culture and tourism are intended to enhance the economy by providing jobs to Saudi youth, who make up the majority of the population. Saudi Arabia has a population of 36 million, of which 36.7 per cent are between the ages of 15 and 34. Until recently, the high unemployment rate among Saudi youth has been a challenge. Statistics now show that the Kingdom's investment in cultural and entertainment enterprises is fostering job creation and lowering unemployment, which fell by 9.7 per cent in the second quarter of 2022.[12] According to a statement released by the Museums Commission, the building of new museums will help achieve Vision 2030's goal of creating more than 100,000 new jobs in the Kingdom.[13]

Riyadh Art, Saudi Arabia's first ever national public art initiative, exemplifies the aim of bringing art to all people in the Kingdom. One of four grand projects conceived by the Royal Commission for Riyadh City, a government entity separate from the Ministry of Culture, its aim is to transform the Kingdom's capital into a dynamic and cosmopolitan city through yearly public art festivals like Noor Riyadh – launched in March 2021 and named after the Arabic word for light – while beautifying the city through the placement of hundreds of public artworks.

'From lower-class neighborhoods to higher- and middle-class districts, everyone gets to live with these sculptures for three weeks', said Jumana Ghouth, the Saudi co-curator of the second edition of Noor Riyadh. 'You are almost forcing society to live with art which will obviously provoke shifts in the way people view the world around them.'[14] The first edition featured works by international artists, including Dan Flavin, Urs Fischer, Ilya and Emilia Kabakov and Yayoi Kusama, displayed next to works by Saudi artists, including Rashed AlShashai, Manal AlDowayan, Maha Malluh and Ahmed Mater, among others. Its goal was to offer all Saudi residents and visitors art to see and experience.

'In the beginning there were individual efforts to integrate art into the Kingdom', adds Ghouth. 'The fact that there is a dedicated festival with a massive budget to annually integrate over 82 public sculptures by both international and local artists in Riyadh is incredible. We went from a country that doesn't have an art history class in our schools like other countries do, to a festival dedicated to one medium, which is light, and integrating it into the urban landscape of Riyadh.'

There is also the Misk Art Institute (MAI). Established in 2017 as an arm of Mohammed bin Salman's non-profit Misk Foundation, it aims to empower and foster local artists through residencies, mentorships, education, exhibitions and scholarships. 'We have a collective role in Saudi Arabia to fuel the Vision 2030 projects and initiatives', says Nawaf Alharbi, Acting Strategy and Development Director of Misk Art Institute. In January 2020 the MAI reopened the biggest fine arts gallery in Riyadh at the Prince Faisal bin Fahd Fine Arts Hall. It serves as a communal space for artists and creatives offering a library, residency area and an exhibition space. 'Our aims are to always be close to the community and to listen to them and understand what kind of conversations they wish to discuss', adds Alharbi.[15]

Among the new projects garnering the most international attention are the events, initiatives and exhibitions taking place in the ancient desert region of AlUla, located in the Madinah province, under the Royal Commission for AlUla (RCU), a Saudi state commission established in 2017. These include Desert X AlUla, the California-founded exhibition of monumental Land Art, which opened its first edition in AlUla in January 2020 led by Neville Wakefield (see Chapter 4); the upcoming Contemporary Art Museum, AlUla; and the Museum of the Incense Road and numerous other projects under AlUla's Journey Through Time Masterplan, encompassing 15 new cultural assets, spanning galleries, museums and cultural centers.

There are also the Kingdom's numerous 'giga projects' involving culture, tourism and entertainment. These include Diriyah Gate, the new development northwest of Riyadh situated around the UNESCO World Heritage Site of At-Turaif, the first capital of the Saudi dynasty; and The Red Sea Project, a land and property megaproject managed by the Red Sea Development Company, in development along Saudi Arabia's Red Sea coast, announced in July 2017 and calling itself the 'world's most ambitious regenerative tourism project'. When completed it will encompass an archipelago of over 90 islands, and miles of desert and mountain landscapes with hotels and other tourist attractions. The Red Sea Project also includes Amaala, named after the Arabic word for 'hope', a land and property megaproject focusing on luxury tourism aimed at attracting visitors to the Red Sea coast.

Another giga project is Neom, the US$500 billion Saudi smart city being built in Tabuk Province in the northwest of the country as the world's first hyper-connected cognitive city. Neom's name is derived from two words: the first three letters from the ancient Greek prefix *neo*, meaning 'new', and the fourth letter from the abbreviation of the Arabic word Mostaqbal, meaning 'future'. Plans for Neom were first unveiled by MBS in 2017. The Line, a smart linear city in Neom, currently under construction, will be another world-first attraction in the Kingdom, notably for its avant-garde design which will have no cars, streets or carbon emissions. It is yet to be seen if The Line, dubbed by many as a skyscraper that stretches for 75 miles, can live up to its ambitions, which are on par with those of the Egyptian pyramids in terms of grandeur, build, scale and technology. When completed, it will be the world's largest structure, with two buildings up to 1600 feet tall, running parallel for 75 miles, traversing mountains and deserts as a part of a futuristic development to transform the Kingdom.[16]

The list of Saudi Arabia's grandiose projects, new museums and events is endless and ever-changing. Yet within the Kingdom's push for a new modern identity is a quest to preserve, safeguard and uphold Saudi Arabia's cultural heritage, especially the history of the Kingdom's founding and its rise into statehood.

The soft undulating curves and commanding presence of the 18th-century mud-brick structures of At-Turaif – the archaeological trove of royal palaces, mosques, homes and defensive towers of the First Saudi State (1727) – easily tempts visitors to journey inside. Located in Diriyah, a town on the northwestern outskirts of Riyadh, the now carefully restored remnants that were once part of an imposing and powerful city continue to tell the tale of Saudi Arabia's founding. Protected since 2010 as a UNESCO World Heritage Site, the birthplace of the Kingdom is the jewel in the crown of Diriyah. By revitalizing it, Saudi Arabia is also writing the next chapter of its history. 'Our intention is to connect all Saudis to this rich heritage, recreating an important part of Saudi history, and for it to become one of the world's greatest gathering places', says Gerard 'Jerry' Inzerillo, CEO of Diriyah Gate and a world-renowned hospitality and tourism visionary.[17] Inzerillo was appointed by MBS in June 2018 to be the first CEO of the newly created Diriyah Gate Development Authority (DGDA), a US$40 billion development project aimed at restoring and reimagining the ancestral home of the original Saudi state.[18] Upon completion, it is estimated that the development will add 27 billion Saudi riyals (US$7.2 billion) to the Kingdom's GDP, attract 27 million visitors and employ over 55,000 people.[19]

In Diriyah, the new JAX creative district is funded by the state. Within, however, is a growing group of private galleries, artist studios, creative hubs, fashion brands and the Diriyah Biennale Foundation. Launched in 2021, JAX is now home to over one hundred warehouses housing creative spaces. Also underway is a permanent museum in Riyadh dedicated to artists' interpretation of the history of oil. Called Black Gold Museum and scheduled to be completed by 2024, it will narrate the history of oil from prehistoric times to the present through over two hundred works of contemporary art and will be inaugurated in partnership with the King Abdullah Petroleum Studies and Research Center (KAPSARC) at the center's headquarters in Riyadh.

As cultural, art and entertainment events and institutions continue to be rolled out at rapid pace in the Kingdom of Saudi Arabia, there is a good chance that by the time this book is printed, dozens more will have been added, all demonstrating this relentless drive by Saudi Arabia to capitalize on its historic past and the talent of its present-day creatives to usher in a new era.

3

Cultural Tug of War in the Gulf and the Unique Case of Saudi Arabia

In around 2010 a new battle began in the Middle East. It wasn't a battle fought on frontlines but a battle for cultural power, and it was fought, and continues to be fought, in the Gulf states or, to be more precise, in the GCC (Gulf Cooperation Council). In the years following the 2009 Green Revolution in Iran, the Arab Spring uprisings of 2011 and the rise of the Islamic State, the Middle Eastern art scenes in Beirut, Damascus, Baghdad, Tehran and Cairo were overshadowed by the rising powers of the Gulf, awash in money from a decade-long oil boom.[1]

While Kuwait, followed by Bahrain, are recognized as the Gulf nations having the oldest art movements in the Arabian Peninsula, with Kuwait being the first Gulf country to grant scholarships in the arts as early as 1936, and Bahrain developing its own modern art movement during the 1950s with the establishment of the Arts and Literature club in 1952, it was in Qatar and the United Arab Emirates that glittering cultural projects began during the early 2000s. While the traditionally conservative Gulf monarchies of the United Arab Emirates and Qatar have long been invested in cultural development, this new decade witnessed a surge in cultural spending with billions of dollars funneled into splashy new museums, art exhibitions and art commissions. These were driven by a yearning for prestige, artistic enrichment and education, and an early desire to diversify the economy through culture. But now there is a new player in the Gulf culture game: Saudi Arabia. The Kingdom is investing in culture and art on its own terms and in a way different from that previously witnessed in other Gulf states.

The appearance of new art institutions and museums, separate from the national museums that had opened in the Gulf post-independence from Great Britain, began in 2008 in Doha, Qatar, with the opening of the I.M. Pei-designed Museum of Islamic Art. It was followed in 2010 by Mathaf: The Arab Museum of Modern Art, also in Doha. Until then, there had been few centers for modern and contemporary art in the Gulf apart from the Sharjah Art Museum in the United Arab Emirates, inaugurated in 1997. Mathaf marked a turning point and the rise of one of the region's and the world's greatest art patrons: Sheikha Al-Mayassa Al Thani, the sister of Qatar's ruling Emir Tamim bin Hamad Al Thani and daughter of the Emir Hamad bin Khalifa Al Thani, known as the 'Father Emir'. Both the Museum of Islamic Art and Mathaf are run by Qatar Museums (QM), a Qatari government entity that oversees most museums and cultural institutions in the country. Sheikha Al-Mayassa has an estimated annual budget of more than US$1 billion to spend on art for her museums and galleries.[2] Her goal wasn't just to beautify the country, but also through art to change the way the world views Qatar. 'We are revising ourselves through our cultural institutions and cultural development. Art becomes a very important part of our national identity', she said during a 2014 TED Talk.[3]

As Qatar poured billions into culture, its neighbor, the United Arab Emirates, was doing the same, but in a different way. The announcement in 2007 that the Guggenheim and the following year the Louvre were building museums on Abu Dhabi's Saadiyat Island set the course for the United Arab Emirates' grand push for cultural might in a region that until then had very few museums. The Louvre Abu Dhabi, which opened in December 2017, was part of a US$27 billion tourist and cultural development on Saadiyat Island.[4] As in Qatar, the state is directly involved in these institutions: the Louvre Abu Dhabi and the Guggenheim Abu Dhabi (the latter is scheduled to open in 2025) are overseen by the Abu Dhabi Department of Culture and Tourism. Both are national museums of the United Arab Emirates. Dubai, on the other hand, has a more robust private sector comprising commercial art galleries as well as the Art Dubai fair, which has been running since 2007.

'The marketplace is the differentiating factor', says Qatari businessman, art collector and patron Tariq Al Jaidah. 'When people compare Qatar to Dubai, I say the rulers of Dubai are building a corporation and the rulers in Qatar are building a nation.' Dubai, as Al Jaidah points out, also created Art Dubai, a commercial art fair, and tried, he says, 'to compete on that front' – in other words in the marketplace rather than in a mission for nation-building.[5]

How, then, does Saudi Arabia compare to the cultural agendas of other Gulf countries? The major difference between the plans of Doha, Abu Dhabi and Dubai compared to those of Riyadh has to do with a specifically aimed societal impact implemented on a national level and across all sectors of Saudi society. 'What is happening in Saudi Arabia is a national activation with the establishment of a ministry and 11 commissions with cultural, political and economic impact', says Saudi art dealer and collector Mohammed Hafiz. 'What is happening in Saudi Arabia did not happen in Doha, Dubai, or even Abu Dhabi. We have a population north of 30 million people', he adds, arguing that similar developments in other Gulf nations were primarily geared to outside audiences, but that Saudi developments are driven by and directed at the country's own population.[6] Al Jaidah agrees: 'Saudi came onto the scene a bit late and at first it was due to private initiatives like Athr Gallery and Edge of Arabia.'[7] But then, he says, there was the 'great awakening', referring to the opening of the Kingdom and its massive socioeconomic plans.

It goes without saying that for political regimes in the Gulf countries, such grandiose development in the cultural sphere uses art to wield soft power and compete for cultural dominance in the region. But while such an assertion may be particularly true when it comes to Qatar and the United Arab Emirates, what we are seeing in Saudi Arabia is different, especially in terms of scale and impact. Vision 2030, and the specific establishment of a Ministry of Culture with its various commissions and plans for new museums, constitutes a blueprint not just for government patronage of the arts but for the extension of culture and art into every corner of society, with the overarching aim of changing minds and perceptions, and opening the country after decades of closure and harsh conservative Islamic rule. Neither Qatar nor the United Arab Emirates ever experienced closure to the world.

Saudi Arabia also differs vastly from its Gulf neighbors both in size and GDP. With a land area of approximately 2,150,000 km^2, the Kingdom is the second largest in the Arab world after Algeria. Qatar and the United Arab Emirates are much smaller in size, 11,571 km^2 and 83,600 km^2 respectively. In 2022 the Kingdom's population was 36 million; Qatar's was 2.9 million, and the United Arab Emirates' 10.2 million, in both cases made up primarily of expatriates. Qatari nationals, for example, make up less than 15 per cent of the country's total population. In 2022 the Kingdom of Saudi Arabia had a GDP of US$1.5 trillion compared to the GDPs of the United Arab Emirates and Qatar of US$501 billion and US$249 billion respectively.

Such statistics provide the context for the Kingdom's goal of enhancing a thriving indigenous culture. The UAE and Qatar have long catered to their predominantly foreign population and influx of tourism, even if both nations, like Saudi Arabia since Vision 2030, have extensive nationalization programs and infrastructure in the realm of culture. Their cultural plans, especially that of the United Arab Emirates, have been focused on replicating Western cultural institutions.

Critics like Hans Ulrich Obrist, a Swiss art curator, author and director of London's Serpentine Gallery, have argued that Doha takes a different approach from Abu Dhabi by aspiring to a new model that does not 'copy existing models or replicate Western museums, but acknowledges local difference'.[8] Undoubtedly, the vast and expensive cultural missions of both Gulf powers, Qatar and the United Arab Emirates, underline a quest for cultural dominance and diplomacy in a region that had hitherto never been known for its art but just for its oil and conservative brand of Islam. However, some cultural analysts attribute the rapid rise in Saudi's global image and cultural prowess also to the help of western players. As one Middle East-based curator said on condition of anonymity, 'Saudi is spending money at mostly American and British consultants in an unprecedented way.'

In contrast with the United Arab Emirates and Qatar, Saudi Arabia is mobilizing its own cultural resources and artists, of which there are a greater number due to the country's larger population. However, as an anonymous Gulf-based curator states: 'The UAE and Qatar have undertaken advanced institutional efforts far beyond any national effort to support local artistic talent.' This in turn, they explain, has led to numerous scholarships, jobs, public art commissions and an increase in art exhibitions and events in both countries. What is taking place in Saudi Arabia at a state level is new.[9] The Kingdom wants its own artists to engage in conversations with the international art world taking place in the Kingdom, through art exhibitions and events that mix Saudi and international artists, as well as abroad. 'There are many other young, intelligent, grassroots artists coming from very different classes of Saudi society, with training in different fields', noted Chris Dercon, now the new Managing Director of Fondation Cartier in Paris and former Tate Modern Director, stating how 'the Saudi art scene is one of the strongest emerging movements of the Middle East'.[10] While Saudi Arabia, like the United Arab Emirates and Qatar did before it, is now also importing big name Western art brands, such as the recent Centre Pompidou deal to develop a new museum in AlUla, it is at the same time striving to enhance its already established grassroots art scene, and its ancient and modern heritage.

An urgency also grips Saudi Arabia's culture drive not witnessed in either Qatar or the United Arab Emirates – but neither nation endured the history of harsh fundamentalist Islam like Saudi Arabia. Qatar and the United Arab Emirates do have their own set of homegrown galleries and institutions. For example, in contrast to Abu Dhabi, Dubai, which draws wealth from finance instead of the oil reserves located in

Abu Dhabi, has established institutions such as the Museum of the Future, an incubator for futuristic innovation, and the Etihad Museum, which preserves and displays the heritage of the United Arab Emirates. In Qatar, in addition to Mathaf and the Museum of Islamic Art, there is Msheireb Museums and the National Museum of Doha designed by Jean Nouvel. The former celebrates Qatar's heritage houses while the latter reveals Qatari history and culture through traditional, modern and contemporary art. The culture race continues. In March 2022 Sheikha Al-Mayassa announced that Qatar would build the world's largest museum of Orientalist art titled the Lusail Museum, to be designed by architect Jacques Herzog of Herzog & de Meuron, and home to the world's most extensive collection of Orientalist paintings, drawings, sculptures, photography, rare texts and applied arts. It will also establish Art Mill, a campus built at the site of a historic flour mill offering exhibition and performance galleries for modern and contemporary art; and the Qatar Auto Museum, designed by Rem Koolhaas of OMA, presenting 430,000 ft^2 of permanent galleries tracing the evolution of the automobile and how it has influenced the culture of Qatar.[11]

What all three nations have in common in their respective culture drives is their desire to diversify their economies away from reliance on hydrocarbons. Each Gulf monarchy is also invested in varying scales and degrees in the betterment of their societies. Culture has become one of their forms of nation-building, a way to enrich the identities and lives of their citizens, residents and visitors. While the large-scale museums and institutions that have shot up in the desert sands of Saudi Arabia will certainly, like those of its Gulf neighbors, showcase cultural power and foster tourism, they also constitute a different kind of cultural transformation. What is being implemented through vast and meticulous cultural and artistic programming at the highest levels strives to foster societal change at its core by transforming minds and perceptions and educating a populace that until recently had little access to such artistic attractions. The budding Saudi arts scene, which builds upon the preexisting, largely privately funded arts scene, has been brought under formal government direction and institutionalized to support the Kingdom's broader socioeconomic transformation as outlined in Vision 2030. No other Gulf country pegged their grandiose schemes for cultural development to such a carefully structured plan for social transformation.

'The centers of culture in the Middle East used to be Cairo, Beirut, Damascus and Baghdad, but over the last 50 years, with oil wealth having hit the Gulf starting with the cultural boom in Kuwait, hundreds of thousands of young people have been sent abroad to be educated and they have become very well-traveled as a population, much more so than the Arabs of Egypt and the Levant', observes Ali Shihabi, Saudi Arabian author and commentor on Middle Eastern politics and economics. 'While their world took a nosedive economically and politically, the Gulf has been stable and growing for 75 years.'[12] Shihabi believes that the world has never seen such a fast-paced push for societal change through culture as exhibited by Saudi Arabia.

Since its inception in 2018, the Ministry of Culture has produced annual reports, replete with statistics, on all segments of cultural production in the Kingdom, across art, literature, fashion, design and architecture. These reports are carefully studied to evaluate the development of Saudi Arabia's cultural sphere. The goal, says Maha Al-Senan, is to 'use art and culture as a soft power – a way to forge our own artistic and cultural voice and share it both nationally and internationally'.[13] As she observes, 'Art in its modern style in the Kingdom does not reflect the evolution of traditional art in Saudi Arabia, and was highly influenced by Western practice.' Part of the Ministry of Culture's aims is to re-identify and invigorate traditional art and heritage in the country, alongside modern and contemporary Saudi art. Al-Senan explains: 'The way the Western world introduced the history of art made the local populace question their own traditional art practices. The teachers from Palestine and Egypt who came to teach art here were from colonized countries that were influenced by the West, so they taught modern art in accordance with the Western concept, not according to their own local concepts.'[14]

As the great Roman statesman Marcus Tullius Cicero once said, 'Not to know what happened before one was born is to be always a child'. Cultural development in line with the Kingdom's Vision 2030 reform agenda aims not just to create expensively produced museums, institutions, art exhibitions and entertainment. It is about laying the groundwork for a genuine appreciation of past and present Saudi heritage, an appreciation that lays the foundations for the construction of a national identity through art and culture.

Part of the Ministry of Culture's aims, as Al-Senan emphasizes, is to redefine what Saudi culture is in distinction to ideas imported from the West. It is to recall what it means to be Saudi through the country's history, heritage and art. Hence, the large-scale plans to develop the area around Diriyah; and the mission to fully document the Kingdom's art history, uphold heritage sites, both ancient and modern throughout the country, and introduce young Saudi children to the flourishing contemporary art being produced inside and outside the Kingdom through initiatives like Noor Riyadh under Riyadh Art.

The art patronage the world now sees in Saudi Arabia is largely new. At the time of publishing this book, Saudi Arabia is historically unique, at least in the modern era, as the only nation on earth that is investing billions of dollars in the growth of its sociocultural landscape and it is doing so as much to enhance its populace as to maintain and grow its global standing. As one anonymous Arab curator stated: 'Saudi Arabia is a superpower and it cannot afford to collapse. It is a member of the G20, among other roles and holds the balance of the entire region in its hands.' Saudi Arabia's cultural tug of war needs to be won not just for the nation's own benefit but arguably for the greater Gulf and Middle East region. In so doing, it lifts the region and assimilates it with a new global order.

4

A Delicate Balancing Act: Art Creation Amid Unpredictability of the State

It was June 2019 in Basel, Switzerland, and in the 'Unlimited' section for monumental works of art at the 49th edition of Art Basel, a long line of people with eager yet perplexed faces waited to enter what appeared to be an unassuming makeshift white structure with a pale, yellow awning over the front door, reminiscent of what you'd find on an ice cream parlor. Stares were cast at the visitors who had gone inside and walked out with shocked expressions. The artwork was titled *The Safe*. It was made by Riyadh-based Saudi artist Abdulnasser Gharem (discussed in Chapter 1). The work was being sold at Galerie Nagel Draxler for US$600,000. Through hidden, obscure and poignant messages, Gharem's work was an allusion to the controversy surrounding the murder of Saudi journalist Jamal Khashoggi not even a year prior at the Saudi embassy in Istanbul on 2 October 2018. It was criticized as being opportunistic and sensationalist by Saudis, international art professionals and even Art Basel employees.[1] 'It took advantage of a hideous moment through art and shocked everyone, but it was brave', said one Middle Eastern art professional on condition of anonymity. It was a risky work for Gharem too, based to this day in Riyadh where it is strictly forbidden to mention Khashoggi's name in some circles.

Gallerists and friends at Art Basel whispered their concerns for Gharem's safety while the artwork was being written about and analyzed by journalists. Gharem went back home and has continued to create his art, while running Gharem Studio, an independent art center in Riyadh encouraging individual thought and self-expression. Gharem's work is rarely found exhibited publicly in his home country – either in privately or state-supported exhibitions. 'The role of dialogue now is to let people understand', says Gharem.

> I am not trying to force anyone to take my opinion; I want people to understand so that we can be equal. Each artwork has a speech; it's a visual speech with its own story and the purpose of that speech is to let the people come up with their own statement. This is the purpose of an artist today. Art is a way to offer another form of perception.[2]

Liberation of Thought Amid a Carefully Coded Art

Artists in Saudi Arabia have long had to tread a fine line, since any questioning of religious or temporal authority poses a risk to the creator and must, for safety, be veiled in symbolism and metaphors. That is where the freedom lies, as many artists and gallerists in the Kingdom will say, in obscurity, which inherently makes the art more intellectually and visually engaging, akin to trying to a solve a puzzle. Still, the codes provide clues and at times they are more direct than others, which, during the Kingdom's more conservative period up until a few years ago, left the spectator to question why some artworks had been allowed to be shown publicly when others hadn't. It was often a mystery.

Gharem's *The Safe* is a clever work of art. Hidden messages are relayed through phrases, signs, symbols and objects. The work doesn't offer a straightforward condemnation of Khashoggi's killing. The name 'Khashoggi' is not mentioned even once in the artwork. 'Freedom needs to happen first inside the minds of the people', Gharem says. 'We need these kinds of thoughts to help people develop and educate themselves.'

But freedom of thought, he explains, is different from freedom of expression, 'because you can code it through your art', which preserves the integrity of the artist's free thought even if its result is masked in coded messages.[3] 'The freedom of expression carries consequences here', said an anonymous Saudi artist. 'Why would you push things too far? You're wasting your life.'

The Safe is made in Gharem's signature contemporary style with nods to conceptualism – a stylistic preference, whether deliberate or unconscious, which most Saudi artists work in today. The viewer must work to understand the inherent messages and story of a work of Conceptual art, even if they might first feel them through the aesthetics of the work. Ultimately, as Gharem explains, what gives meaning to a work of art lies in the viewer's perception of the work not that of the artist.

Does this style allude to instances of self-censorship or pure artistry? It can be a mixture of both. 'We have a little censor inside of all of us', says artist Mohammed Al Faraj from Al-Ahsa in the Eastern Province. 'I believe in the old way of maneuvering, of using metaphors and symbols – these are the tools of poetry and of code. Institutions and the society are more tolerant if you speak in metaphors and in symbolism.'[4]

While religious restrictions are more relaxed, there have been and still are no set rules as to what is permissible to show publicly. It all depends on the party that is in power and approving the works of art, which is now the Saudi state. 'A good challenge makes for good art; a structure that is disruptive and obstructive allows artists to really think hard about how they are working and what they are trying to say and also makes an audience so much smarter', says artist Manal AlDowayan.[5] As Mohammed Hafiz, collector and co-founder of Athr Gallery puts it:

> Yes, there are women driving and there are musicians playing, but as for the artists and their practices, the practice remains the same. There is now a larger space for artistic expression and a

> large number of new opportunities. [But] I believe that the so-called restrictions have forced artists to think outside the box. When you are an artist here, you find your voice in between these restrictions.[6]

In 2005 AlDowayan produced her famous *I Am* series of silver gelatin print black-and-white photographs capturing Saudi women working as doctors, scuba divers and petroleum engineers. The photographs, whereby AlDowayan shows part of each woman's face or portrays them donning the traditional metallic face mask worn by women in the Gulf as they pose next to items from the aforementioned vocations, poignantly react to the restrictions imposed upon women in Saudi Arabia. The photographs were shown in 2006 in an exhibition space in Saudi Aramco and subsequently with the British Council's *Common Ground* exhibition at Riyadh's King Fahd Cultural Center.[7] 'Politicians and religious figures in Saudi Arabia have, for years, hijacked the dialogue on women's rights', wrote AlDowayan in 2005 as an explanation of the series on her website. 'They have turned women's right to work in a public sphere into an issue that threatens Saudi identity, the structures of family, and the religious principles that underpin Muslim society.' When the series was created, less than 3 per cent of Saudi women were formally employed. Today that number has risen to over 35 per cent.[8]

AlDowayan argues that self-censorship in some respects is a concept created by the West. 'The art I created is a reflection of the world around me and how I grew up', she says, stating how she never deliberately tried to conceal subjects in her art. AlDowayan's work, in black-and-white photography, sculpture, video, sound, neon and large installations, responds to the cultural and religious ambiance in which she was raised on the Saudi Aramco compound in Dhahran, a major city in Saudi Arabia's Eastern Province. A particularly edgy work by AlDowayan for the time it was made was her 2011 installation *Suspended Together*. It comprises 200 porcelain doves, onto each of which is plastered a permission document from her male guardian allowing a woman to travel. Dozens of Saudi women donated their permission documents for AlDowayan to create the work. *Suspended Together* is an example of a work that is indirectly critical of the previous male guardianship system that the present King Salman abolished in 2017. The work was not censored. Censorship, states AlDowayan, was not state-implemented, but influenced by Saudi societal norms, and 'then people took it upon themselves to implement it'.[9]

In another case, however, Riyadh-based artist Abdullah Al-Jahdhami, known as Shaweesh, had his work of Saudi American track and field athlete Sarah Attar, whom he portrayed running with a sword while carrying the Saudi flag, censored in 2014 during a show at the former Ayyam Gallery in Jeddah. He says he doesn't know why it was censored. 'Maybe because it portrayed an empowered woman', he muses.[10] Although, today, he adds, after advancements for women in Saudi, it is unlikely it would be censored. 'What is the point of a good work if the artist is banned?' asks Shaweesh. 'The way you deliver the work is important and this is done after you are finished with the concept, idea and research. The main idea of a work of art is the core element and its execution is totally different.' The presentation of a work of art, he further explains, is where you deal with possible censorship, but no matter what the final aesthetic product of the work is, 'it must remain true to its idea, message, and it has to say it', he adds, citing the story of Perseus, the slayer of Gorgon Medusa, in Greek mythology. 'If Perseus looked into the eyes of Medusa, he would have died, so he used her reflection in a mirror so he could fight. You need to know how to speak to the people in a way that they will turn what you are saying into a discussion without offending anyone.'[11]

The predominant contemporary style in which Saudi artists work today is one that has survived, persisted, evolved and garnered much international attention for its edgy disruptive power cloaked in carefully construed codes, striking a balancing act between real and perceived messages and intent. These are the works that the Saudi Ministry of Culture is now championing. 'I thought none of the works I make would ever make it into public institutions in my own country, but they have, and I tell museum directors that the work is critical, and they say they want it', says AlDowayan. 'Their response is an indicator that there is a huge transformation. We are ready to reconcile our history and discuss it and debate it through art. It's wonderful.'[12]

Paradox at the Heart of Saudi Art Creation

There is a paradox at the heart of MBS's grand transformation plan for Saudi Arabia: vast social and economic change has taken place in parallel with what journalist Ben Hubbard calls 'an extreme concentration of authoritarian power'. 'His rise has been dominated by two simultaneous drives that will continue into the future', writes Hubbard in *MBS: The Rise to Power of Mohammed bin Salman*, continuing:

> MBS's Saudi Arabia is a place where women can drive, work and travel, but where campaigning for more rights can mean jail time. It is a place where young people can mingle and ride rollercoasters and launch start-ups, but where questioning the wisdom of government policies is considered treason. It is a place where young women can entertain dreams forbidden to their mothers and grandmothers, but where law-abiding citizens fear that talking to journalists or human rights groups could make them disappear.[13]

In August 2022 Salma al-Shehab, a 34-year-old PhD student at Leeds University in the UK, was charged with following and retweeting dissidents and activists, thereby spreading 'false' rumors. She was sentenced to 34 years in prison followed by a 34-year travel ban. Al-Shehab was also a lecturer at Princess Nourah bint Abdulrahman University in Riyadh and the mother of two sons.[14] A few days later, another Saudi woman, Nourah bint Saeed al-Qahtani, was sentenced to 45 years for using Twitter to express her opinions, convicted of 'using the internet to divide society' and 'undermine public order'. She had been detained in the Kingdom since 2021.[15] In October 2022 Saudi American Saad Ibrahim Almadi, a 72-year-old retired project manager, was sentenced to 16 years in prison over tweets he sent while in the United States that were critical of the Saudi government.[16] He was neither a dissident nor an activist. He was released in March 2023.[17]

In March 2022 Saudi Arabia's Ministry of Interior announced it had executed 81 men on one day, including one Syrian national and seven Yemenis, on account of 'multiple heinous crimes'. Lynn Maalouf, Amnesty International's Deputy Regional Director for the Middle East and North Africa, said in a statement that 'Saudi Arabia's deeply flawed justice system metes out death sentences following trials that are grossly and blatantly unfair'.[18] While the situation in Saudi Arabia is problematic, it is important to note, in this context, that human rights abuses persist in other parts of the world, notably China which Amnesty reported executed thousands of people last year. At the end of 2021, according to Amnesty, at least 28,670 people were known to be under sentence of death worldwide.[19] The United States also continues to administer the death penalty, with approximately 4 per cent being wrongly convicted.[20]

Several artists working in Riyadh and the Eastern Province, who asked not to be named, said the recent imprisonments have generated more 'fear' among creatives. Others disagree, stating that they feel less controlled in the absence of the hawk-like watch of the religious or 'morality' police, the once-feared Mutawa, tasked with enforcing Islamic law, who were banned in 2016, and who used to examine and approve every work of art before it went on show.[21] However, the state, through the Ministry of Culture, still plays a large role in determining which works of art will be exhibited. For every exhibition that is supported by the government, which means most art events in the Kingdom given the miniscule private sector of just a handful of galleries and very few collectors (further explored in Chapter 5), the Ministry of Culture must approve the artwork and the concept of an exhibition or event before it is staged.

MBS's efforts on the social front are groundbreaking, nothing short of revolutionary, and this is where the paradox lies. For an entire generation of Saudi youth, life will be undoubtedly richer. But it is government ministries, particularly those of art and education, that are working to make this happen.

Other recent news signals that times have indeed changed. On the evening of 22 August 2022, the unthinkable happened. Artist, curator and poet Ashraf Fayadh (discussed in Chapter 1) was set free from a Saudi prison after eight years and eight months, during which time, for nearly three months, from 2015 to 2016, he was under a death sentence to be administered by beheading. He was arrested in August 2013 by the religious police after a man reported that in 2011 Fayadh had made a blasphemous remark in a cafe in Abha, a city in southern Saudi Arabia. After a global media uproar and protest by the international art community, Fayadh's death sentence was overturned, yet he was sentenced to eight years with 800 lashes to be delivered over 16 sessions. Fayadh's treatment deeply disturbed the Saudi art world. 'When I heard that Ashraf had been let free, I was stunned', said Riyadh-based artist Halla bint Khalid. 'This would have been impossible, unthinkable just a few years ago.'[22] Saudi artist Ahmed Mater said that times have changed and that what happened to Fayadh is unlikely to happen today.[23] Others remain fearful, lacking trust in the recent rapid changes amid the ongoing crackdown of dissent. 'None of us know what is going on, what we will wake up to and what new laws there will be that will fundamentally change the way we go about things', said bint Khalid. 'These are not subtle changes. We don't really know how to step and where to step. We are all confused.' Another young photographer who recently graduated in 2020 from engineering school in Riyadh says he and his fellow classmates were told upon graduating to delete their Twitter and Facebook accounts. 'The change is external, what you see around you every day; but it hasn't happened on the inside of society yet', he said on condition of anonymity.

Regardless of the rapid change and its effects, artists are producing just as they did before during times of extreme restrictions, and arguably more so now given the increase in new-found state-sponsored opportunities. 'Many more opportunities, institutes and residencies championing art creation in Saudi Arabia are opening up new avenues for artists who are younger and not yet known', said a young Saudi artist who requested to remain anonymous. 'Communities are being built, allowing other artists and emerging artists to explore their own mediums and voices.'

The Struggle to Be Seen and Heard Amid a Reductionist Geopolitical Lens

Critics have branded the Kingdom's 'cultural revolution' as a 'propagandistic' and 'artwashing' attempt to divert attention from human rights violations, Khashoggi's murder and the (US-supported) war with Yemen. Following Khashoggi's killing in 2018, there was a series of boycotts and protests – including the cancellation by New York's Columbia University of a talk by Ahmed Mater scheduled to take place the same month as the journalist's assassination.[24] The boycotts and protests have continued, and Saudi artists are often put in the position of having to defend their art against the state's unpredictable actions.

Desert X's decision to host an inaugural edition in AlUla in January 2020 led several board members to resign, and *Los Angeles Times* art critic Christopher Knight to call the event 'morally corrupt'.[25] Despite the uproar that it caused, Desert X marked the first major international art event of its kind in Saudi Arabia. Its second edition, held in February 2022, opened to a gentler, more accepting tone, with international guests and prominent art-world figures flying in for the opening weekend. The organization still faces backlash for its decision to show in Saudi Arabia, with the Palm Springs City Council declining to sponsor a Desert X installation in February 2021 over concerns about the biennial's Saudi edition. 'I think it's unfortunate that they went to Saudi Arabia, with their track record of human rights abuses . . . I would like to see Desert X continue in the city of Palm Springs, and that they can reform their ways and stop partnering with human rights abusers', said Christy Holstege, Mayor of Palm Springs, during a board meeting.[26]

Her concerns echo the stream of calls to boycott cultural and entertainment events in the Kingdom as MBS's grand transformation plans continue to roll out. In December 2021 Justin Bieber performed in Saudi Arabia despite public pressure for him to boycott because of 'human rights abuses'. Journalists, too, even those with many years of experience in the region, have often been caught in the crossfire when writing on culture in Saudi Arabia for Western media. 'In some cases, I felt I had to navigate between the editorial line of the Western outlet while focusing on the art events on the ground', says Melissa Gronlund, an American arts journalist who has covered the Gulf for years.[27]

Critics believe Saudi Arabia's cultural revolution is merely a means to veil its heinous human rights track record.[28] 'Saudi Arabia, along with its allies in the region and the United States, continues to eradicate Arab life, most blatantly in the culture rich nations of Iraq and Yemen', wrote California-based writer and arts practitioner Rijin Sahakian in a piece for *Hyperallergic* titled 'A Coalition of The Willing: How Saudi Arabia and US Arts Institutions Partnered on a Cultural Diplomacy Offensive'.[29] The article was written after the murder of Khashoggi and in response to the barrage of Saudi state-sponsored art and cultural events taking place at the same time. Sahakian says her thoughts have not changed. 'To believe their state-sponsored creative platform can live apart from this violence is just one demonstration of how the catastrophes of the Iraq and Yemen wars are sanctioned through both the military and art worlds – which depend most critically on access to capital and the manufacturing of legitimacy.'[30]

While Saudi Arabia's cultural opening has surprised the West, there are good reasons to bet on its achievements and its potential to foster creative, economic and intellectual growth, particularly for its young population. Moreover, an engagement with and openness to Saudi art and culture offer a means to better understand the complexities of Saudi past and present history. Art provides a window into the Kingdom's long and greatly misunderstood culture and nourishes the ability to better understand its social realities and how its populace has grappled with decades of change amid the establishment of their modern state. Art has the capacity to show the everyday and human side of a society that has often been viewed through a reductionist lens of political and religious rhetoric.

‘Those who argue about whitewashing are thinking that everything Saudi Arabia does has the West in mind and that the West is at the center of everything that is happening, which is typical of Western narcissism’, said Bernard Haykel, Professor of Near Eastern Studies and Director of The Institute for Transregional Studies at Princeton University. ‘While there might be some elements of that, I think it is principally being done for domestic reasons and not for external consumption.’[31] Kristin Smith Diwan, Senior Resident Scholar at the Arab Gulf States Institute in Washington, notes however that ‘it is understandable why some people view these efforts as “artwashing”’. She asserts that the Saudi state ‘is now deploying a heavy hand in its embrace and promotion of these creative fields. It is becoming harder to find the independent space between the state and the artists. And the leadership is eager to publicize these new achievements abroad as evidence of Saudi Arabia’s new direction.’[32]

In cafes throughout the Kingdom, at major events and in shopping malls, change is palpable. Young filmmakers now shoot in the streets of Jeddah where just a decade ago they would have needed to dodge the religious police. And Saudi creatives who emigrated during the Kingdom’s ultra-conservative period have now returned, eager to participate in the cultural revolution as if to make up for lost time. The sky seems to be the limit for Saudis wishing to flex their creative and business muscles.

But the Kingdom’s culture plans go beyond even cultural and social change. ‘Saudi Arabia’s social and cultural reforms are a bet on survival’, says Haykel, who believes that sociocultural changes, catering largely to the youth, aim to completely transform the state and the society to secure the ‘survival of the regime. These changes are not just to shock or entertain or whitewash in the West; they are driven by a realization that the country as it was previously constituted politically and economically is unsustainable and that diversification of the economy and the social opening of society must be taken seriously.’[33]

New creative and entertainment endeavors in the Kingdom have generated national pride. But does a top-down approach to culture equate with propaganda, as the Kingdom's critics would have it? Is art being fostered with a political agenda? Most Saudi artists will tell you no. They are not told to create art around certain subjects with specific formal qualities. Some artists, however, criticize the present scene, because, in their view, it fails to recognize a plurality of artistic voices. 'No one can deny that the cultural exchange that has begun to take place between Saudi Arabia and the world is a huge step forwards', says Gharem. 'Particularly by creating new infrastructures and platforms that will enrich and generate a dialogue between the arts and the public. It seems, however, that the artists as well as the presented subjects are strictly controlled.'[34] Foreign art specialists are now working in the Kingdom, such as British curator Iwona Blazwick, former longtime Director of London's Whitechapel Gallery, who was appointed in July 2022 to chair the Royal Commission for AlUla's Wadi Al Fann or 'Valley of the Arts' as translated from Arabic. Blazwick believes, as reflected by Vision 2030, that creativity will foster an economic change that is greatly needed in the Kingdom. 'It is not a society that has a culture towards innovation or entrepreneurship; it's very passive and very orthodox and until people have access to creative thinking or models to look at, the society cannot move away from this reliance on oil', she explains.[35] In her new role Blazwick is overseeing the installation of a series of site-specific works amid a 25-square-mile portion of AlUla. The five artists contributing to the inaugural Land artworks are Ahmed Mater, James Turrell, Michael Heizer, Agnes Denes and Manal AlDowayan (see Chapter 6), to be unveiled by 2024.[36] 'The West sees everything from its own perspective', notes Blazwick, adding that:

> The term artwashing is so lazy. Art is art. It is not instrumentalist wherever it happens, whether in America, China or Russia. When people say they must boycott cultural events in Saudi Arabia, how will that change anything? If you aren't part of it, if I can't share my experience and my expertise with women in that region, then nothing will change.

Gharem is one of several artists who believe Saudi Arabia is undergoing a 'harsh enlightenment', the outcome of which remains unknown and which he thinks is done largely to project a new image of the Kingdom to the West. Still, within this period of cultural enlightenment, regardless of the rapid pace at which artists are being pushed to create and museums to open, Vision 2030's forceful wave of cultural creation has given many creatives hope and belief in the change they have desired for decades. As artist Muhannad Shono says, 'I feel like people had secretly changed a long time ago, maybe it's a generational shift, we were just waiting for walls to fall so we could collectively step back into the sunlight'. He adds: 'Through an opening of the cultural scene and the lessening of social restrictions, change is happening on a cellular level. Individually, there is an embrace of hope. And that has changed everything.'[37] Despite the unpredictability of the state, and the myriad new laws being passed, amended or entirely abolished, there is undoubtedly a state of hope and a new urgency among Saudis, particularly the young, to express themselves through creative discipline, to open and engage more fully with the world, and to enjoy a newfound pride in their Saudi identity.

5

State-Controlled Cultural Production, Art-World Infrastructures and A Nascent Private Sector

At its core, Saudi Arabia's social transformation has a principal aim: fostering a new creative economy separate from oil and gas to usher in a new era of tourism and economic development. This can only be done, as MBS has understood, by changing the Kingdom's society. Through the Kingdom's grandiose development plans, investment in creative sectors and efforts to reform its education system, the comparatively small private creative sector is also witnessing gains. Most of Saudi Arabia's art dealers affirm that sales of art in the Kingdom, particularly for work by Saudi artists, have increased since the Ministry of Culture was created in 2018. Challenges, however, remain. A stifling and rapidly changing bureaucracy, and a regime that has continued to crack down on dissidents in tandem with its opening up of society, breed what Kristin Smith Diwan of the Arab Gulf States Institute in Washington calls 'a dissonance limiting the expression of the new Saudi Arabia that the state is trying to present to the world'.[1]

Cultural diplomacy has become a byproduct of Saudi Arabia's social transformation. While practiced for centuries, cultural diplomacy is still a relatively new concept. It refers to the exchange of ideas, information, art and other cultural products to forge mutual understanding among nations. In its aim to attract and collaborate rather than coerce, soft power goes together with cultural diplomacy. According to Joseph Nye, former Dean of Harvard's Kennedy School of Government, who coined the term during the 1980s, soft power arises from the attractiveness of a country's culture, political ideals and policies.[2] Nye suggests that a country's image on the world stage is vital to its ability to enact soft power, and that is exactly what Saudi Arabia is betting on through its culture drive and massive social reforms.

Vision 2030 is making changes at home through the reforms already mentioned in this book, including the growth of a diversified economy, international tourism and the empowerment of women and youth, as well as creating new investment opportunities – all part of what is deemed a successful foreign policy strategy. 'We [Saudis] were bombarded with a negative image from the world for decades of only having oil and terrorists', says Ohoud Al-Najran, a Saudi woman passionate about Arab art and culture who previously ran O Gallery in Riyadh. 'And now the government is showcasing the beauty of our art, culture, heritage and traditions to the world.'[3] Members of the Saudi art scene state that what Saudi Arabia is witnessing is no different from countries like France, which also invests heavily in its art and culture. Cultural diplomacy is thus an organic outcome of a country's cultural vision. For example, in his first speech as UK Prime Minister on 25 October 2022, Rishi Sunak vowed to fix the UK's image.[4] 'All countries want to forge a good image on the world stage', says Mohammed Hafiz.[5]

There are, however, several constraints to the Kingdom's top-down approach to cultural expansion, an approach that simultaneously encourages artistic growth but which its critics say poses a risk to individual artistic expression and identity. Let us see why.

Monopolized Art Production

The instrumentalization of art for cultural diplomacy can impact both the practice of the artists making the art and the art being produced – the very resource that Saudi Arabia needs to successfully work its magic for cultural diplomacy. 'Let us hope that today's centralized organization of art and culture, with the patronage and support of the Saudi government, does not tamp down the energies, ambitions, and achievements already set free', Chris Dercon wrote in the catalogue of *Feeling the Stones*, the first edition of the Diriyah Biennale.[6] In 2020 Dercon became a founding member on the boards of the Visual Arts Commission and Museums Commission under the Saudi Ministry of Culture.

As previously stated in this book, art in Saudi Arabia at present is largely, if not almost entirely, funded by the state. At the time of writing, there are only around four to five commercial galleries for modern and contemporary art in the country. These include Athr Gallery, cofounded by Mohammed Hafiz and Hamza Serafi in Jeddah and considered one of the Kingdom's pioneers in actively promoting contemporary Saudi art internally and abroad since it opened in 2009 (see Chapter 2); Mono Gallery in Riyadh, which opened in 2018; Hafez Gallery in Jeddah, open since 2014; Lakum Artspace in Riyadh, established in December 2021; and Naila Art Gallery in Riyadh, running since 2012. There are a few small, local commercial art fairs in the Kingdom, including the annual Shara Art + Design Fair in Jeddah, which launched in 2015 as Jeddah's first commercial art fair staged by the Saudi Art Council (SAC). It now attracts a mix of both regional and Saudi art and design galleries and includes a silent auction and a fair, with the proceeds going to support the operations of SAC.[7] Misk Art Institute also staged an art fair as part of Misk Art Week in 2019 with local and international galleries participating.

Operating a commercial art gallery in the Kingdom, in the absence of a strong cultural sector, has been a challenging task, particularly before the recent social reforms. Former contemporary art galleries in the Kingdom included Lam Art Gallery, which opened in 2010 and closed around 2018, and O Gallery, which was opened in October 1997 by Al-Najran (cited above) and closed in 2008 due to the financial challenges of running the gallery. Al-Najran was a pioneer at the time. She traveled the Arab world scouting for artists from the Levant and North

Africa who could show their work in the Kingdom alongside works by Saudi artists. 'My goal was to expose art to the people of Saudi Arabia during a time when there wasn't much art', she says. 'I used to sell works for several hundred to several thousand Saudi riyals to people throughout Riyadh.'[8] She adds that it was the artists who set their own prices.

Athr Gallery, particularly under its cofounder Mohammed Hafiz, is taking on an increasingly hybrid role within the Saudi art scene, one that straddles the private and government sectors. For a short period in 2021 Hafiz worked at the Ministry of Culture. The founding Vice Chair of the nonprofit Saudi Art Council, he was also then briefly the Chair of the organization before it was disbanded. One of SAC's primary sponsors has been the Ministry of Culture since the latter was established in 2018.[9] Athr began participating in blue-chip international fairs, including Frieze London in 2021, Art Basel Hong Kong in 2016 and Art Basel in Basel in 2022, and has participated at Art Dubai since the fair's inception in 2010, but the gallery's biggest client at present is the Saudi state. Due to increased demand, including from government commissions, the gallery set up Athr Agency in 2019. Athr's artists are now among those most regularly exhibited in the country's state-led art events. While it maintains its gallery in Jeddah, Athr has opened several new spaces in the Kingdom, including in the JAX creative district in Diriyah in Riyadh; and in AlUla – in March 2022 it opened Athr Gallery AlUla in the city's new AlJadidah Arts District. Lastly, during Volta Basel in June 2022, the gallery launched Athr Foundation, a nonprofit foundation that supports independent Saudi-based artists. 'Five years ago, there was none of this and these commissions wouldn't have happened', says Hafiz. 'You have an opportunity now if you are in the sector, if you are an artist, gallerist, consultant or curator. All the Saudi curators I know are hired now. Five or seven years ago these people were jobless and now they are among the most in demand human capital in the Kingdom.'[10]

Aarnout Helb, a Dutch art collector and lawyer, began collecting Saudi art in 2008 to better understand the Kingdom's culture after the events of 9/11 and the wars in Afghanistan and Iraq, because he 'felt those wars were counterproductive in bringing people together again'. He says he is concerned about the Saudi state's increasing control of the art scene. 'I think there is a huge future for people in Saudi Arabia to make art and to enjoy it', adds Helb, who established the Greenbox Museum of Contemporary Art from Saudi Arabia in Amsterdam in 2008. 'In terms of this period now, I am a bit worried that everything is being done by the government and that everybody starts catering to that. You need an independent scene composed of galleries and artists.'[11]

A Saudi art professional, who spoke on condition of anonymity, agrees that there is an inherent risk to the type of art being created when the state is monopolizing artistic production, despite the government's good intentions. 'I am concerned that the way the governmental sector is directing the artwork targets more what they want rather than representing the unique style and vision of the artist', she says. 'When the people know that this is the direction, immediately everyone shifts their artistic vision to cater to what the government wants because this is where the money, power and target is.' Saudi artists, on the other hand, state that when they are commissioned, they are left free to create as they wish. 'We discuss the concept a bit, they make suggestions but then I am free to create as I want', said Mohammed Al Faraj, a self-taught artist and former engineer from the Eastern Province represented by Athr Gallery.[12] His work commissioned by the Visual Arts Commission at the Ministry of Culture offered a critique of the fast-paced changes of Saudi Arabia's present transformation.

Before 2017 and the government's spending spree on culture, young Saudi artists were able to develop their work at a slower pace, showing primarily through private local initiatives, strongly rooted in Saudi civic society, through Athr Gallery and 21,39 art festival organized by the Saudi Art Council, which was funded by private patrons only, both in Jeddah. Prior to the government's involvement due to Vision 2030's aims, these initiatives had no geopolitical goal, but aimed to discover, support and connect young Saudi artists, both locally and internationally. There is no denying that the Saudi state's upper hand on cultural creation, while providing opportunities to many, has shifted the pace of artistic creation and prompted private entities to become embroiled with its aims and messaging too.

In terms of public institutions, there is one player that stands out as a wholly non-governmental entity: Art Jameel. 'We exist independently, with thanks largely to Jameel family philanthropy, and work collaboratively with a range of partners, locally and globally', says Antonia Carver, Director at Art Jameel. Carver says Art Jameel has been focusing on supporting the Kingdom's younger, up-and-coming artists whose work is more interdisciplinary. 'Our mandate in Saudi Arabia is to help broaden access to the arts and to create opportunities for practitioners to engage in long-term research and considered thinking', she adds. 'It's incredibly exciting what's happening now and to be celebrated, but a diversity of approaches seems important. Encouraged by and responsive to the community, we strive to provide something of a counterweight to the current fervor, fueled both externally and internally.'[13]

Apart from Art Jameel and Ithra – the King Abdulaziz Center for World Culture (see Chapter 2) built by Saudi Aramco – all major art commissions in the Kingdom at present are led by the government and its respective bodies dedicated to culture to support Vision 2030 plans.[14] Artists are working around the clock to create special commissions, such as the large-scale light installations for Noor Riyadh, the annual public art show staged under the auspices of Riyadh Art. As under the Medici in Renaissance Florence, successful Saudi artists are making money largely through the state. 'Where is government not bureaucratic?' asks Hafiz. In the case of Saudi Arabia, he says, 'you are spending public money to create art for the society. We have made more money as a gallery than we did three years ago.' For Hafiz, that is proof that the top-down approach is working to foster the private sector. 'The government has created immense demand by putting up projects like the Diriyah Biennale which cost millions. Every gallery has an artist that participated in these events.'[15]

The British cultural entrepreneur and artist Stephen Stapleton, who co-founded Edge of Arabia in 2003 and continues to work in the Kingdom, says that,

> the Saudi artists we exhibited as part of Edge of Arabia between 2008 and 2018 put critical thinking at the center of their practice; they expressed a tension and a conflict that was an honest reflection of the society they were trying to change. That language doesn't feel as relevant now as it did then, mainly because of the significant changes that are taking place in Saudi's cultural sector. When you have 500,000 people dancing at a festival on the outskirts of Riyadh, all expressing themselves in a way not publicly seen before in this country, the darker psychological symbols – of fear, of conflict – which were so evident in the best Saudi art of my generation don't make as much sense as they used to.

Stapleton explains that he finds the artwork made after 2018 to be not as powerful, not as original, as the works made during the early 2000s. 'It's still important for the artists here to be radical and I think there is a challenge now in that the arts ecosystem is more focused on commissions, fast delivery and the language of consultancy and that isn't a context in which artists necessarily thrive, nor feel free', he says. 'But I am also not a big fan of the private sector model from my society – the Western art fair, auction and gallery model, for example, which is so connected to the financial systems of the West and the use of art as an asset class within the investment sector. That is not a true art economy in the sense that it is not coming out of art makers.' Stapleton adds, however, that there is an interesting opportunity now for Saudi artists to be radical but without 'fear and conflict at the center of their practice'. He also sees some artists unable to produce in this new environment. 'I would ask them', he muses, '"Are you afraid or are you simply not able to keep up? Not able to produce work that you feel is authentic at this speed?"'[16]

What will encourage more artists to produce in Saudi Arabia?

During this period of rapid change, investment from the government needs to be translated into genuine artistic innovation. It takes time to develop a new language, one that reflects on the current era of Saudi Arabia rather than the past. Neama Al-Sudairi says that she founded Lakum Artspace to encourage a creative community in Riyadh. While there has been a lot of progress because of government support, there is still room, she notes, for further improvement. 'What is difficult for us is that sometimes artists don't respect our agreements with them, and when they get approached directly by potential clients, including government entities, they sell to them directly, leaving us in a challenging position', she notes. 'Hopefully this changes as the government starts to encourage artists to work with galleries to build a sustainable private sector which is necessary for the growth and ecosystem of any art scene."[17]

Advisor to the Ministry of Culture Maha Al-Senan explains how the ministry believes that through government investment it can encourage a flourishing private art sector in the Kingdom. 'We are building the market by investing in the scene and encouraging that the art and infrastructure produced is Saudi made', she says, adding that the ministry is also encouraging other government entities to buy Saudi art through set guidelines for the acquiring of art from Saudi Arabia rather than from galleries in London or Dubai. 'We are helping investors and business owners to be sustainable so in the long term they don't have to rely on the government for the next 10 to 15 years.' In research she conducted in 2014, Al-Senan noted even then the possibility of attempting 'to develop strategic priorities', by 'emphasizing the role of the public sector, represented by the Ministry of Culture and Information, in ensuring the identity of Saudi contemporary art, finding marketing venues, and culturally sustaining it as a local economic product'.[18]

While the state might be able to jumpstart a local art economy and signal its importance to the people, it is up to Saudi artists, creatives, collectors, patrons and gallerists to take the initiative. However, as various art professionals have noted, with most aspects of the art scene being monopolized by the state, there is little room to maneuver independently. 'The current situation raises another key question: How mutual is the artistic dialogue between the Kingdom and other geographical areas, both in the region and abroad? How might such exchanges impact the Saudi art of the future?' Dercon asks in his essay for *Feeling the Stones*. 'Whatever the answer may be, such a dialogue cannot be forced or purchased; infrastructure alone is not sufficient. It is, at its core, a very slow process of carefully planned, multivalent perspectives, one which requires a vision beyond cultural diplomacy. Without these, Saudi art will remain open to misinterpretation and conjecture.'[19]

To establish a flourishing art scene, with multiple actors, takes time. As Kristin Smith Diwan rightly notes:

> When looking at this dramatic shift, it is important to judge it from where Saudi Arabia was before rather than just judging it on its own right now. When you look at Saudi Arabia, its art scene is uniquely placed, not only by the former very traditional conservative environment, which is one that you find across the Gulf, but by a very specific religio-politico formation that militated for a long time against any kind of creative expression.[20]

A Miniscule but Growing Collector Base

The other constraint for the growth of a private sector in the Kingdom is a lack of collectors. At the time of writing, most of the art buying is done by the state or by a few wealthy individuals and art patrons. The Saudi art sector has hitherto developed without the market and with social engagement as its driving force. It now, and increasingly, will have to reckon with huge market forces, as demand will likely swing upwards as the country's art scene garners more visibility abroad. While this is a very real possibility in several years' time, specialists at auction houses such as Sotheby's and Christie's state that Saudi collectors are very seldom, if at all, present at auction, but do note an increased interest in art from Saudi Arabia proven by a growing secondary market.[21]

Representatives from the handful of private galleries affirm that the Ministry of Culture's investment is encouraging the growth of a local collector base. Mo Ali, Managing Director at Hafez Projects, a subsidiary of Hafez Gallery in Jeddah, set up in 2019, says that since the government's massive investment in culture, they are finding more Saudis buying Saudi contemporary art and 'Saudi investors exporting Saudi art abroad'.[22] Mono Gallery, which participates in notable regional fairs, including Art Dubai, MENART in Paris and Shara Art + Design in Jeddah, and sells work by artists from Saudi Arabia, the Gulf region, North Africa and the West, has also noticed an increase in sales from Saudi collectors over the last two years.[23] The market, says Hafiz, is more competitive. 'All the global players are coming to Saudi Arabia now. Everyone is bidding for the RFPs [Request for Proposals; explored further in Chapter 6]. Sometimes you win the commission, sometimes you lose.'[24]

In response to increased demand from the state and private sector, however, some galleries appear to be inflating prices, portraying an art market bigger than the present reality in the Kingdom. Several foreign art professionals have noted the challenges Saudi artists are having today when it comes to pricing. Prince Badr, the Minister of Culture, is supporting artists often by buying their work, but the prices he is paying, says a source, are not commensurate to where the artist is in their career. 'Galleries and also artists are inflating prices and certain individuals are buying the art at very high prices because they want to support the arts, which creates the illusion of an economic reality different from what it really is', says the source. 'Prices are increasing and there is a lot of demand on art being purchased between the UAE and Saudi now, with both governments trying to support their artists, which has contributed to a rise in prices', said an anonymous Dubai art dealer.

Collector Aarnout Helb notes that price inflation is nothing new to the Gulf. 'From as early as 2008 it has been taking place', he says, calling it a 'price paradox' that is the result of 'real Gulf opportunities versus international realities'. However, inflated prices for Saudi artists were the reason, he says, why over the last ten years several larger museums did not buy artwork by artists from the Kingdom, even after looking for loans and Saudi sponsors. 'They thought prices for young artists were much too high', he explains, adding:

> Naturally, these prices seem to work sometimes in the very affluent Gulf area. That is the self-defeating victory they have. It might be you then cut out of business not only international parties, but also younger, less wealthy, Saudis who might collect otherwise. I am not sure. It's not only prices that are inflated, the number and sizes of editions, are sometimes also a bit much.

With the increase in cultural expenditure from the state generating an increased interest among the Saudi populace and foreigners who come to the Kingdom, prices and competition for Saudi art and among galleries are indeed beginning to rise. As Helb puts it: 'Perhaps more wealthy Saudis may start buying in this changed environment. That could also be a reason for upward pressure on prices.' But as various gallerists in Saudi have noted, affluent Saudi men with a fleet of expensive cars are still wary of paying serious money for an artwork. 'If such men become inspired by Vision 2030, who knows, they may start buying art from Riyadh instead of cars from Germany', remarks Helb.[25] However, various sources in Riyadh and Jeddah note that such potential collectors need to be educated by more than just a few galleries and by a healthy secondary market on what to buy – and not to buy – with their money.

The biggest collecting institutions based in the Kingdom include the two private non-governmental entities of Art Jameel and Ithra, and the government's cultural bodies, such as the Royal Commission of AlUla (RCU), the Ministry of Culture and the Royal Commission for Riyadh City (RCRC). The state-led bodies are building their own collections by commissioning and buying artists' work from the country's miniscule gallery sector. While times are quickly changing, and the Saudi market is growing, selling an artist's work for an exorbitant price when they are just beginning their career could prove detrimental to that artist's market down the line, particularly when they begin to sell outside the country. A perfect example is what happened to Chinese artists during the Chinese art market boom of 2006 to 2007. Artists one year out of college were selling works for as much as US$10,000 each.[26] But when the market crashed in 2009, it left artists scrambling to adjust their prices abroad.

Preserving Artistic Authenticity

Artists and cultural practitioners in the Kingdom are questioning how to navigate the slippery realm between state and private sponsorship while staying true to their own artistic voice and identity. 'We need to look at the saturation taking place right now in the scene and ask if it is too much and too fast', says Saudi artist and curator Moath Alofi. 'We need more collaboration between state-sponsored platforms and independent platforms and artists to understand what we are trying to achieve as a scene as a whole.' Alofi emphasizes that what is evident is that 'we are building something for the future. But we don't know how it will look in the next five to ten years' time, but I am sure it will be unique and interesting.'[27]

Those Saudi artists who are now being commissioned frequently by the government lament of being overworked, exhausted and pressed to create new commissions for the state under extremely challenging deadlines. 'By 2030, the artists and creatives who have relied entirely on the support of government projects will face emptiness and lack of opportunity', Al Faraj says. 'This is why I encourage my friends to work on other commissions, take opportunities from different places, wherever, do something else, create your own ecosystem as an artist to rely on different modes of income and work.'[28] Other artists struggle to get their work exhibited in Saudi or abroad if they haven't been commissioned by certain government bodies, unless, of course, artists wish to exhibit outside the country. 'It is up to the Saudi people themselves to take the initiative and build the private sector', says artist Sultan bin Fahad.[29] Al Faraj agrees, stating that it is up to the artists to choose which commissions they take, 'to say yes to what feels right for them, and no for the ones that are not, and to take their own initiative, and they need to do so as their responsibility as cultural workers, to not be burnt out, maintain their originality but more importantly to open a space for other artists too'.[30]

The Ministry of Culture is also sponsoring an art school, to open in JAX. While studying art history and specific artistic genres is paramount for Saudi artists, particularly inside the country where there are still no art schools apart from basic art classes in primary and secondary school and university, one area, largely self-taught (apart from those who studied abroad), which Saudi artists will tell you they desire to study is art economy. Like all artists, they want to know how to support and represent themselves while making a sustainable income and continuing to produce high-quality art.

Joseph Nye's notion of soft power in its purest version is challenged in the context of Saudi Arabia because the government's rapidly changing policies and political ideals may make the outside world question the motives behind the Kingdom's cultural drive. But the Kingdom's support of the arts can lay the foundation for a true cultural diplomacy that will come from the integrity and vision of the Saudi artists themselves.

6

Engaging with Saudi Arabia's New Arts Playing Field: Opportunities and New Perspectives

How does the world, particularly the West, engage with Saudi Arabia on a cultural playing field? In the geopolitical and media realm Saudi Arabia's culture drive is often subject to criticism in the West, and negative stereotypes. But amid the Kingdom's hard-to-rationalize contradictions between cultural and social transformation through radical reform and a tightening of authoritarian rule, cultural practitioners, media, artists and academics continue to flock to Saudi Arabia, attracted by the opportunities for art and culture created by the government's massive expenditure. Those who choose to do so often navigate a difficult terrain. They are caught in the crossfire between praise and condemnation in their home countries and the unpredictable nature of Saudi bureaucracy during this moment of rapid and radical change in the Kingdom. But the challenge of attempting to understand and work within this complex landscape attracts those who, including the authors of this book, continue to have the Saudi people at heart.

The cultural realm could offer a space in which to understand each other, despite historical differences, beliefs and traditions, and where commonalities and mutual respect can be forged. This, in essence, is what constitutes a road to soft power. But can one ever separate culture from politics? No. Over the last decade, particularly in Europe and the United States, works of art, exhibitions and cultural events are sharply condemned or praised according to strict partisan perspectives. Rather than engage with the 'other' through cultural enterprises, boycotting has become a favored cultural practice of late, and it happens regularly for the artists and creatives of Saudi Arabia.

In the realm of Saudi politics and their tumultuous relationship with the West, while specialists on Saudi Arabia's economics and political affairs continue to light up debate over the sore wound of dialogue between Riyadh and Washington, little is often said or studied about the Kingdom's culture, which Kristin Smith Diwan believes has shaped its politics and society.[1]

To work in the Saudi cultural sector in 2023 offers a range of seemingly limitless opportunities, not to mention the possibility of engaging with a young and dynamic scene that is quickly expanding through the influx of financial capital and the predominance of Saudi youth eager to explore both their heritage and contemporary culture, and to communicate this exploration to the world. But those artists who do decide to work in the Kingdom must keep in mind the rapidly changing social landscape of the country and its conservative Islamic past, as well as the predominant role of the government, especially the web of bureaucratic protocols for all cultural projects.

Given the rapid rate of change in the country, shifting government policies are to be expected. At present, to do any sort of creative endeavor in the Kingdom can be a time-consuming project, where much energy is caught up in bureaucratic protocols, challenging deadlines, approvals, and applications and payment procedures. A case in point is the predominant use of Request for Proposals (RFPs) for any event or project where state money is involved; the government receives numerous bids for each project before it agrees to allot a certain amount of money. 'One needs an RFP to do anything, for each single entity and aspect of any project or show', said a source at the Ministry of Culture on condition of anonymity. 'To stage any single event related to one of the Ministry's commissions, and also the Diriyah Biennale, an RFP was needed for the strategy company, the food, the build out and the PR.' For creative professionals coming from abroad, eager to engage in cross-cultural dialogue with Saudi artists and contribute to this rapidly developing cultural scene, the RFP makes it challenging for artistic work to take place, particularly at the speed required. 'You can't curate with RFPs', said Neville Wakefield, Desert X Artistic Director and co-curator of the 2022 edition of Noor Riyadh:

> Because government agencies are not equipped to trickle out money, they have these large single-service contracts, which means before they take on any idea for curatorial content, the contract goes first to an event company, often not suited to producing or working with artists, or an exhibitions company, not used to working with museum-quality art, so there is already a dissonance between the art created and the infrastructure to support it.[2]

As Wakefield explains, the curators end up curating to meet the deliverables of the RFP, rather than for the artwork or show at hand. All Saudi cultural bodies have a procurement process that involves RFPs, and some entities are more challenging than others for foreign art professionals, particularly the Royal Commission for Riyadh City (RCRC) that stages Noor Riyadh, because it includes an RFP for the curatorial team, meaning, as one source put it, that curators and other art professionals are treated as vendors. 'Things will prove more challenging as time goes on unless there is a separation of artistic practice from the art industrial complex', adds Wakefield. The eminent Swiss art critic, curator and art historian Hans Ulrich Obrist regularly gets asked to be part of multiple proposals or RFPs because he is approached by consulting companies working in Saudi Arabia who see that he is a famous curator when they search his name online.[3] Within the Kingdom, its cultural ministry, relevant bodies, commissions and functionaries must find common ground to work with international actors and artists to better understand the global art scene and the possibilities for art creation.

An Opportunity for Cross-Cultural Dialogue

It is crucial that those who work in the Kingdom do so with open hearts and minds that value cultural exchange. Saudis have an innate sense that outsiders come to the Kingdom to take, lured by the country's oil wealth and the myriad opportunities on offer now. They are also very aware of the stereotypes with which they have been labeled for years, at home and abroad. They like to feel that there is an exchange – that they will also benefit. For instance, if a foreign arts professional is working with a Saudi artist in the Kingdom, it would be beneficial for the Saudi artist to receive opportunities from the practitioner to show their work outside Saudi Arabia, or to participate in a panel talk at a major artistic and cultural event abroad. Saudi artists, particularly the younger generation, eagerly desire to engage with the world, not just at home.

What cultural collaboration challenges individuals to do, believe many foreign arts practitioners who have chosen to work in the Kingdom, particularly when engaging with cultures so entirely different from their own, is to enter an uncomfortable place where history, ethics and long-held beliefs are often questioned. 'It is important now to separate the people and the artists from the government and the powers that be', said Stephen Stapleton in 2019. 'We are living a very emotional moment. We must never forget what happened to Jamal [Khashoggi] and what he stood for, [just] as we can't forget America's decision to go to war with Iraq.'[4] In the post-colonial world where the centers of world creation and power are at a turning point, cultural engagement, no matter how uncomfortable at first, offers a way to transcend narratives that mold and continue to shape perceptions of that world. To enter an uncomfortable realm, and engage with the 'other', is an attempt, even on a miniscule level, to break patterns of war and economic disparity.

Iwona Blazwick, in her new role as the Chair of the Royal Commission for AlUla's Public Art Expert Panel, overseeing the Wadi Al Fann initiative (referenced in Chapter 4), joins a team commissioning permanent artworks in AlUla, providing a lead for modern and contemporary art in the region. 'The way these projects are being curated has ethics at the forefront', she says, continuing:

> For the Land Art commissions, as well as celebrating the great pioneers, we want to reflect artists from the region, the Global South and beyond. The first five artists include Manal AlDowayan and Ahmed Mater, both rising stars of the Saudi art scene alongside established, iconic figures Agnes Denes, Michael Heizer and James Turrell. I think it's significant that a mid-career Saudi woman is being given the same prominence and resources as a very established artist like Turrell. It is an important project because it reflects a shift in the geopolitical axis away from the dominance of the North American and European narrative. We are approaching it from the Gulf but also from Africa, Asia, South America – there are great artists from the Global South that we need to pay attention to and that have been overlooked in the canon of modern art. This marks a paradigm shift in artistic discourse.[5]

Blazwick also emphasizes the twofold opportunity of her role to work with the heritage and environmental preservation of AlUla. 'This initiative is a very carefully choreographed way of reiterating and echoing the legacy of the Nabatean era while also ensuring that artists create works in harmony with the local ecosystem', she says. 'We are inviting artists to work in a way that respects the ancient heritage of this area and the surprisingly rich animal and plant life of the desert. It's also important that artists engage with local communities.' AlDowayan's project involves the direct participation of these communities. Her work garners the stories of individuals residing in the ancient adobe settlement of AlUla and incorporates them into her sculpture. 'Other artists will act as mentors to emerging creatives from the region; or offer training in the fabrication and management of permanent art works', Blazwick adds. 'Our commissioning process must be reciprocal and inclusive.'

Blazwick has defended her new post in light of the country's record on human rights, stating: 'I'd rather be involved where I can help contribute to freedom of expression, to art being nurtured, because I believe art changes society. That's fundamental to who I am. And it's fundamental to my support for women throughout my career', she says.[6] 'If you are interested in human rights, then surely you must be interested in change. And I know that there's a huge suspicion and a skepticism about whether art is used in a purely emblematic way. But what I'm seeing is systemic change at an institutional level, [such as] art and culture being brought into the [Saudi] school curriculum.'[7] Engaging with Saudi Arabia's art scene offers a chance to transcend cultural divides and polarizing Eastern and Western narratives. Neville Wakefield believes that engaging with Saudi Arabia's cultural sphere is about creating platforms for artistic voices that have yet to be heard.

Courage, compassion, and an open mind and heart are required then, when working in cultures different from one's own, but regardless of the challenging contexts which can be found in regions and nations worldwide, the ability to work with creatives in a country with a growing art scene offers a chance to forge new realities, narratives and ideas, and to contribute to a greater change in society and the world. 'The more difficult the context, the more important it is to engage and to be present and empower those who are determined to challenge the usual structures of power', says Wakefield. 'The reason everyone wants to do this, the artists and myself, is to open up dialogue. The common voice among all the artists I've been working with has been, "If you don't give people the opportunity to change their hearts and minds and become engaged with outside cultures, then you're part of the problem, not part of the solution."'[8]

Conclusion

Saudi Arabia's New Creative Economy

Against the endless, arid landscape of the harsh Saudi Arabian desert, a man in a white thobe – the traditional Saudi male dress – approaches a camera swiftly, with fierce determination, almost as if his life depended on it. He carries with him a paintbrush dripping with crude oil. An eerie feeling of violence fills the scene as the man, Saudi artist Nugamshi (b.1982), takes his paintbrush and after making a few calligraphic marks, smashes the glass and his painting. Titled *Sarab*, which means 'mirage' in Arabic, the work was made in 2016, the year Vision 2030 was launched, and was included in *Naphtha*, an exhibition curated by Moath Alofi at Khuzam Palace in Jeddah, organized by the Ministry of Culture during the summer of 2019.[1] To this day the film stands out as a provocative representation of the changes taking place in the Kingdom, the shock-and-awe effect of breaking with the past to usher in a new social and economic reality. Nugamshi's work also evokes the frustration, confusion and even anger of Saudi Arabia's youth, their desire to break free from both the blessing and curse of the Kingdom's oil wealth and its impact on their personal and collective identity.

In this book we have attempted to capture a specific moment in time as Saudi Arabia continues to undergo intense and rapid change in its society and economy in tandem with a government that has tightened its grip through its authoritarian rule. We have looked at this particular period through the voices of Saudi artists within the context of the drivers of Saudi politics and economics. We don't know what the Saudi Arabia of 2030 and afterwards will look like, nor do Saudi artists or creative professionals. Many, however, do feel that this period of intense state investment in the arts, despite its long-term commitments, is temporary, hence the urgency to take advantage of the moment – a moment unlike anything Saudis have seen before, given that not even ten years ago there were almost no opportunities for creative expression. 'I think that by 2030, this influx of money and resources towards art and culture will be cut down a lot and it will be targeted to something else, most likely to alternative energy, which for me makes sense', said artist Mohammed Al Faraj. 'But this change will create turbulence because now there are a lot of opportunities for the creative sphere and suddenly these opportunities will be less, and the money will be targeted to something else.' But until 2030, the creative sector is a priority area of focus for the Saudi government. As has been repeatedly stated in this book, to create an economy separate from oil, people's minds need to be opened, new ideas need to be fostered, and this all happens, as the Saudi regime has understood, from creative thinking. 'I think art can change ideas', adds Al Faraj. 'You need creative ideas to make something like The Line [discussed in Chapter 2].'[2] As Hussein Ibish, Senior Resident Scholar at the Arab Gulf States Institute in Washington, wrote in 2022: 'The Saudi leaders know that they have merely a few decades left of major oil revenue in which to use hydrocarbon resources as the basis for a transformation to a viable post-hydrocarbon economy. This is urgent, risky and cannot be postponed.'[3] And hence comes the Saudi version of a creative economy, jumpstarted with the Kingdom's oil revenue.

Is a creative economy being built in Saudi Arabia? Most certainly. Yes, the funding for the Kingdom's cultural revolution is coming from the government, but as we have sought to demonstrate, government spending is fostering great investment of time, energy and money in a growing network of individuals and businesses from the private sector that are already functioning and profitable in the Kingdom. This in turn is beginning to expand Saudi Arabia's own private creative sector – the seeds of which were sown decades ago when there was little government support. The catch, however, is this: Can you have a thriving creative economy when basic civil liberties are still controlled? Art scenes that have thrived under communist China and under Tsarist Russia similarly demonstrate that a vibrant art scene coupled with enriching creative thought can exist even within societies where authoritarian rule does not grant total freedom to its people. Is the art that is made, as in the case of Saudi Arabia, affected? Yes. But the artists, as Mohammed Al Faraj has put it, are used to operating with the 'censor inside'. They have learned the art of metaphor and symbolism and embrace it wholly and, in their belief, it does not detract from the message they are trying to convey. Their art cannot be labeled as 'propaganda', as its artistic creation is not propelled by the state, even if its financial production and support is.

The Saudi Arabia of today remains a place of contradictions – often hard to rationalize for the Westerner attached to the ideals of liberal democracy in which individual rights and freedoms are officially recognized and protected – and the exercise of political power is limited. As Maha Al-Senan points out, 'democracy itself is a Western term'.[4] And even in the West the concept of liberal democracy is being questioned, with many people distrusting their governments and the economic order, and urging reform.

While art in Saudi Arabia is undoubtedly influenced by its geopolitical and social contexts of the last century, it also strives to break away from external influences, from Western-imposed narratives, from the religious and social restrictions that influenced it, and to move towards a new aesthetic and metaphorical language, ultimately, as Muhannad Shono's highly conceptual works demonstrate – a new reality conducive to human flourishing.

Saudi Arabia remains a country in motion, one with its recent past very much alive. But it seeks to reform and renew to better survive both as a country and as a regime. Saudi artists' work often retains this uneasy yet urgent dual relationship between the past and the present.

What we hope to show is the urgency among Saudi creatives to have their work be heard and seen at home and abroad. They are eager to move forward while still remembering the past. We still don't know what will be the long-lasting result of Saudi Arabia's grand cultural schemes. Will they make a difference? The change in the short term is palpable and pulsating with urgency, vitality and enthusiasm for young Saudis across the country who have increased purpose, jobs and are brimming with creative ideas and concepts. Still, only time will tell the long-term socioeconomic effects of Saudi Arabia's cultural project. In the meantime, Nugamshi's zealous thrusts, smashing the glass and calligraphic oil painting before him, break through the unsettling and contradictory nature around him, like an art that transcends the chaos, uncertainty and contradictions of daily life. His movements are akin to a collective call to action: Listen to what *we* have to say.

Notes

Introduction: Art as a Catalyst for Social Change in Saudi Arabia

1 Saudi Vision 2030 Overview, https://www.vision2030.gov.sa/v2030/overview/vibrant-society/.
2 Global Economic Diversification Index website, 'The Index', as of August 2023, https://economicdiversification.com/the-index/.
3 Beliz Tecirli, 'Kingdom of Art', *AramcoWorld*, July/August 2022, https://www.aramcoworld.com/Articles/July-2022/Kingdom-of-Art.
4 ibid.
5 Dana Khraiche and Paul Wallace, 'Saudi Economy Grows at Fastest Pace in a Decade on Oil Boom', *Bloomberg*, 1 May 2022, https://www.bloomberg.com/news/articles/2022-05-01/saudi-arabia-economy-grows-at-fastest-pace-in-decade-on-oil-boom.
6 John Howkins, *The Creative Economy* (new edition, Penguin Books, London, 2013).
7 UNCTAD, https://unctad.org/topic/trade-analysis/creative-economy-programme.
8 ibid.
9 Bernard Haykel, interview with Rebecca Anne Proctor, January 2022.
10 Kristin Smith Diwan, interview with Rebecca Anne Proctor, October 2022.
11 Alice Thomson, 'Saudis are realizing the ground didn't open when women started to drive', *The Times*, 16 October 2021, https://www.thetimes.co.uk/article/saudis-are-realising-the-ground-didnt-open-when-women-started-to-drive-g39fsvgbs.
12 Opening of Diriyah Contemporary Art Biennale, 10 December 2021.
13 Rebecca Anne Proctor, '"I am Not Part of Some Propaganda Machine": Artists and Curators Defend Their Participation in the Saudi-Backed Show Desert X

AlUla', *Artnet News*, 29 January 2020, https://news.artnet.com/art-world/desert-x-alula-preview-1763889.

14 Philip Tinari, interview with Rebecca Anne Proctor, 15 February 2022.

1: From Past to Present: The Sources of Saudi Arabia's Culture Drive

1 Artist's website, https://www.ahmedmater.com/artworks/artwork/evolution-of-man.

2 'Saudi Arabia facts and figures', OPEC website, https://www.opec.org/opec_web/en/about_us/169.htm.

3 Ghadeer Sadeq, 'The Saudi Artists Who Paved the Way', King Abdulaziz Center for World Culture (Ithra) website, https://www.ithra.com/en/news/saudi-artists-who-paved-way/.

4 Ghadah Shukri H. Albakri, 'Transforming Art Education in Saudi Arabia: Inclusion of Social Issues in Art Education', Phd thesis, University of North Texas, August 2020.

5 ibid.

6 Diana Elena Lieske, 'Saudi Contemporary Art as a Commentary on the Social Issues Present in the Kingdom of Saudi Arabia in the 21st Century', BA Arabic Dissertation, SOAS, London, 2017, https://www.academia.edu/33802302/Saudi_Contemporary_Art_as_a_commentary_on_the_social_issues_present_in_the_Kingdom_of_Saudi_Arabia_in_the_21st_century.

7 Sherifa Zuhur, *Middle East in Focus: Saudi Arabia* (ABC-CLIO, Santa Barbara, 2011).

8 'Dia Aziz Dia, Saudi artist, sculptor and photographer', *Arab News*, 10 November 2020, https://www.arabnews.com/node/1760836/saudi-arabia.

9 'Saudi Arabia Showcases Contemporary Art', BBC, 3 March 2015, https://www.bbc.com/news/entertainment-arts-31599674.

10 Ahmed Mater, 'The Development of the Saudi Art Scene from 1960', essay for Sotheby's on the artist's website, https://www.ahmedmater.com/essays/development-of-the-saudi-art-scene-from-1960.

11 Lieske, op.cit.

12 Exodus 20:4–6.

13 'A Mayor's Vision and Lasting Legacy', Art Dubai blog, 11 September 2017, https://www.artdubai.ae/blog/a-mayors-vision-and-lasting-legacy/.

14 Bashar Al Shroogi, *Fast Forward* (Saudi Art Council, Jeddah, 2014).

15 ibid.

16 ibid.

17 Moayad Al Rasasi and Waheed A. Banafea, 'The Effects of Oil Shocks on the Saudi Arabian Economy', *The Journal of Energy and Development*, vol.41, nos 1/2

(Autumn 2015 and Spring 2016).

18 'Saudi culture society launches institute for arts and culture training', *Arab News*, 2 October 2018, https://www.arabnews.com/node/1381546/amp.

19 ibid.

20 Ahmed Mater, 'The Development of the Saudi Art Scene from 1960', op.cit.

21 David Commins, *The Wahhabi Mission and Saudi Arabia* (Bloomsbury Publishing, London, 2009).

22 'Saudi Textbook Features Image of Yoda with King Faisal', BBC, 22 September 2017, https://www.bbc.co.uk/news/world-middle-east-41363156.

23 Maha Al-Senan, interview with Rebecca Anne Proctor, September 2022.

24 Halla bint Khalid, interview with Rebecca Anne Proctor, September 2022.

25 Manal AlDowayan, interview with Rebecca Anne Proctor, September 2022.

26 Maha Al-Senan, interview with Rebecca Anne Proctor, October 2022.

27 Mohammed Al Saleem, 'A World for the Sake of Art', in *Modern Art in the Arab World, Primary Documents*, edited by Anneka Lenssen, Sarah Rogers and Nada Shabout (Museum of Modern Art, New York, 2018).

28 Loring M. Danforth, 'Art Evolution: Saudi Arabia', *Utne Reader*, 26 October 2016, https://www.utne.com/arts/art-in-saudi-arabia-zeoz1610zfol/.

29 ibid.

30 All quotes, Filwa Nazer, interview with Rebecca Anne Proctor, October 2022.

31 Ashraf Fayadh, interview with Rebecca Anne Proctor, October 2022.

32 Ali Shihabi, interview with Rebecca Anne Proctor, October 2022.

33 https://www.nysed.gov/news/2021/statement-chancellor-young-board-regents-and-commissioner-rosa-20th-anniversary-911.

34 Abdulnasser Gharem, interview with Rebecca Anne Proctor, October 2022.

35 Maha Al-Senan, interview with Rebecca Anne Proctor, October 2022.

2: A New Saudi Arabia: Art on the Frontlines of Social Transformation

1 Adbulnasser Gharem and Ashraf Fayadh, interviews with Rebecca Anne Proctor, October 2022.

2 Ahmed Mater, 'The Development of the Saudi Art Scene from 1960', op.cit.

3 http://edgeofarabia.com/about.

4 Abdullah K. AlTurki, interview with Alia Al-Senussi, October 2022.

5 Aramco website, https://japan.aramco.com/en/making-a-difference/planet-and-people/ithra.

6 Abdullah K. AlTurki, interview with Alia Al-Senussi, October 2022.

7 Afra Naushad, 'Design, art and education come together at Alaan Artspace', *Arab News*, 21 November 2012, https://www.arabnews.com/design-art-and-education-come-together-alaan-artspace.

8 Qaswra Hafez, interview with Rebecca Anne Proctor, October 2022.

9 'Our Culture, Our Identity: Our Cultural Vision for the Kingdom of Saudi Arabia', Ministry of Culture, March 2019, https://www.moc.gov.sa/en/about.

10 Quote by Ministry of Culture spokesperson for *Harper's Bazaar Art*, Summer 2019, p.36.

11 Ashleigh Steward, 'Saudi Arabia announces details of new film, fashion and music commissions', *The National*, 5 February 2020, https://www.thenationalnews.com/arts/saudi-arabia-announces-details-of-new-film-fashion-and-musiccommissions1.974259#:~:text=The%2011%20new%20bodies%20are,the%20Literature%2C%20Publishing%20and%20Translation.

12 'Saudi unemployment rates drop 9.7 percent in second quarter of 2022', *Arabian Business*, 29 September 2022, https://www.arabianbusiness.com/politics-economics/saudi-unemployment-rates-drop-9-7-percent-in-second-quarter-of-2022.

13 Tamara Abueish, 'Saudi Arabia announces plans to transform, build museums across Kingdom', *Al Arabiya*, 20 September 2021, https://english.alarabiya.net/News/gulf/2021/09/20/Saudi-Arabia-announces-plans-to-transform-build-museums-across-the-Kingdom.

14 Jumana Ghouth, interview with Rebecca Anne Proctor, 5 October 2022.

15 Lujain Al Ubaid, 'Saudi Youth: Leading Change in Arabia', Visit Saudi, 2022, https://www.visitsaudi.com/en/do/culture/youth-culture.

16 Rory Jones, 'Inside Saudi Arabia's Plan to Build a Skyscraper That Stretches for 75 Miles', *The Wall Street Journal*, 23 July 2022, https://www.wsj.com/articles/inside-saudi-arabias-plan-to-build-a-skyscraper-that-stretches-for-75-miles-11658581201.

17 Saudi Press Agency interview, 23 February 2021, https://www.spa.gov.sa/viewstory.php?lang=en&newsid=2194061.

18 ibid.

19 Jonathan Gornall and Lama Alhamawi, 'Diriyah: Past, Present and Future', an *Arab News* Deep Dive, no date, https://www.arabnews.com/Diriyah.

3: Cultural Tug of War in the Gulf and the Unique Case of Saudi Arabia

1 Nadeen Ebrahim, 'Why the current oil boom for Arab states may be their last', CNN, 19 September 2022, https://edition.cnn.com/2022/09/19/business/middle-

east-last-oil-boom-mime-intl/index.html.

2 Allie Jones, 'So the Art World's Biggest Player Is Now a 30-Year-Old Qatari Woman', *The Atlantic*, 23 July 2013, https://www.theatlantic.com/culture/archive/2013/07/art-worlds-biggest-player-30-year-old-qatari-woman/313009/.

3 'Globalizing the local, localizing the global', TED Talks, https://www.ted.com/talks/sheikha_al_mayassa_globalizing_the_local_localizing_the_global.

4 Tamara Walid, 'Unique Plans for US$27bn Saadiyat', *Arabian Business*, 30 April 2006, https://www.arabianbusiness.com/abnews/unique-plans-for-us-27bn-saadiyat-208903.

5 Tariq Al Jaidah, interview with Rebecca Anne Proctor, October 2022.

6 In Rebecca Anne Proctor, '"We have our own individual voices": Saudi Artists Debate Their Place in the Kingdom as the West Becomes Wary of its Commitment to Progress', *Artnet News*, 12 September 2019, https://news.artnet.com/art-world/saudi-arabia-artists-1646848.

7 Tariq Al Jaidah, interview with Rebecca Anne Proctor, October 2022.

8 Quoted in Rebecca Atkinson, 'Eastern Promise', *Museums Journal*, January 2011, pp 29–31.

9 Interview with Rebecca Anne Proctor, 19 September 2023.

10 Chris Dercon, 'What we can learn from Saudi Art', *The Art Newspaper*, 9 April 2018, https://www.theartnewspaper.com/2018/04/09/what-we-can-learn-from-saudi-art.

11 Eileen Kinsella, 'Qatar Announces it will build the World's Largest Museum of Orientalist Art Along with Two Other Starchitect-Designed Institutions', *Artnet News*, 28 March 2022, https://news.artnet.com/art-world/qatar-plans-three-major-new-museums-2090743.

12 Ali Shihabi, interview with Rebecca Anne Proctor, 8 October 2022.

13 Maha Al-Senan, interview with Rebecca Anne Proctor in Riyadh, 25 September 2022.

14 Maha Al-Senan, interview with Rebecca Anne Proctor, September 2022.

4: A Delicate Balancing Act: Art Creation Amid Unpredictability of the State

1 Sources at Art Basel, conversations with members of Saudi and international art community.

2 Abdulnasser Gharem, interview with Rebecca Anne Proctor for *Harper's Bazaar Art*, 2019.

3 ibid.

4 Mohammed Al Faraj, interview with Rebecca Anne Proctor, 27 October 2022.
5 Manal AlDowayan, interview with Rebecca Anne Proctor, October 2022.
6 Rebecca Anne Proctor, '"We have our own individual voices"', op.cit.
7 Mohammed Rasooldeen, 'We are One World, Says Straw', *Arab News*, 19 April 2006, https://www.arabnews.com/node/283492.
8 Mariam Nihal, 'Saudi Arabia: Women in work has "doubled" to over 35% of labour force', *The National News: Gulf News*, https://www.thenationalnews.com/gulf-news/saudi-arabia/2022/05/18/saudi-arabia-women-in-work-has-doubled-to-over-35-of-labour-force/.
9 Manal AlDowayan, interview with Rebecca Anne Proctor, October 2022.
10 Abdullah Al-Jahdhami, interview with Rebecca Anne Proctor, October 2022.
11 ibid.
12 Manal AlDowayan, interview with Rebecca Anne Proctor, 11 October 2022.
13 Ben Hubbard, *MBS: The Rise to Power of Mohammed bin Salman* (HarperCollins, New York, 2020), pp 277–8.
14 Isabel Debre, 'Saudi doctoral student gets 34 years in prison for tweets', *The Associated Press*, 18 August 2022, https://apnews.com/article/saudi-doctoral-student-tweets-prison-sentence-40cc8b2dc8cf7c8322c4cab475c79121.
15 ibid.
16 'Saudi Sentence US Citizen to 16 Years Over Tweets', *The Associated Press*, 19 October 2022, https://apnews.com/article/middle-east-arrests-social-media-united-states-5f6443c63fd2d625f8df741f0238d90e.
17 Marita Maloney, 'Saad Ibrahim Almadi: Saudi Arabia releases US man jailed over tweets', BBC, 21 March 2023, https://www.bbc.com/news/world-middle-east-65022370.
18 'Saudi Arabia: Mass execution of 81 men shows urgent need to abolish the death penalty', Amnesty International, 15 March 2022, https://www.amnesty.org/en/latest/news/2022/03/saudi-arabia-mass-execution-of-81-men-shows-urgent-need-to-abolish-the-death-penalty/.
19 'Death Penalty 2021: Facts and Figures, Global Figures', Amnesty International, https://www.amnesty.org/en/latest/news/2022/05/death-penalty-2021-facts-and-figures/.
20 David Von Drehle, 'More Innocent People on Death Row Than Estimated', *Time*, 28 April 2014, https://time.com/79572/more-innocent-people-on-death-row-than-estimated-study/.
21 Henry Hemming, 'Bureaucracy and Censorship: A Palpable Thaw in Saudi Arabia', *The Art Newspaper*, 1 April 2014, https://www.theartnewspaper.

com/2014/04/01/bureaucracy-and-censorship-a-palpable-thaw-in-saudi-arabia.
22 Halla bint Khalid, interview with Rebecca Anne Proctor, October 2022.
23 Anna Somers Cocks, 'Artist and Poet Ashraf Fayadh is Freed after more than eight years in Saudi Prisons', *The Art Newspaper*, 31 August 2022, https://www.theartnewspaper.com/2022/08/31/artist-and-poet-ashraf-fayadh-is-freed-after-more-than-eight-years-in-saudi-prisons.
24 Helen Stoilas, 'Columbia University cancels talk with Saudi artist Ahmed Mater amid scrutiny over the kingdom's cultural funding', *The Art Newspaper*, 18 October 2018, https://www.theartnewspaper.com/2018/10/18/columbia-university-cancels-talk-with-saudi-artist-ahmed-mater-amid-scrutiny-over-the-kingdoms-cultural-funding.
25 Christopher Knight, 'Why the Desert X art festival deal with Saudi Arabia is Morally Corrupt', *The Los Angeles Times*, 29 October 2019, https://www.latimes.com/entertainment-arts/story/2019-10-29/desert-x-alula-saudi-arabia.
26 Max Stromberg, 'Palm Springs Takes a Stance Against Desert X Biennial's Partnership with Saudi Arabia', *Hyperallergic*, 24 February 2021, https://hyperallergic.com/624095/palm-springs-desert-x-christopher-myers/.
27 Melissa Gronlund, interview with Rebecca Anne Proctor, 5 February 2022.
28 Cathrin Schaer, 'Saudi Reforms: Royal Power Play or Meaningful Change?', *Deutsche Welle*, 27 June 2021, https://www.dw.com/en/saudi-arabia-reform-royal-family/a-58017860.
29 Rijin Sahakian, 'A Coalition of the Willing: How Saudi Arabia and US Arts Institutions Partnered on a Cultural Diplomacy Offensive', *Hyperallergic*, 1 November 2018, https://hyperallergic.com/468850/saudi-arabia-and-us-art-institutions/.
30 Rijin Sahakian, interview with Rebecca Anne Proctor, October 2022.
31 Bernard Haykel, interview with Rebecca Anne Proctor, January 2022.
32 Kristin Smith Diwan, interview with Rebecca Anne Proctor, October 2022.
33 Bernard Haykel, interview with Rebecca Anne Proctor, October 2022.
34 Abdulnasser Gharem, interview with Rebecca Anne Proctor, January 2022.
35 This and subsequent quotes, Iwona Blazwick, interview with Rebecca Anne Proctor, 14 October 2022.
36 'Iwona Blazwick to Oversee Saudi Arabia's Wadi Al Fann', *Artforum*, 5 July 2022, https://www.artforum.com/news/iwona-blazwick-to-oversee-saudi-arabia-s-wadi-al-fann-88788.
37 Muhannad Shono, interview with Rebecca Anne Proctor, January 2022.

5: State-Controlled Cultural Production, Art-World Infrastructures and A Nascent Private Sector

1 Kristin Smith Diwan, interview with Rebecca Anne Proctor, 14 October 2022.
2 Joseph S. Nye, *Soft Power: A Means to Success in World Politics* (PublicAffairs, New York, 2009).
3 Ohoud Al-Najran, interview with Rebecca Anne Proctor, 22 October 2022.
4 'Rishi Sunak's first speech as Prime Minister: 25 October 2022', Gov.UK, 25 October 2022, https://www.gov.uk/government/speeches/prime-minister-rishi-sunaks-statement-25-october-2022#.
5 Mohammed Hafiz, interview with Rebecca Anne Proctor, October 2022.
6 *Feeling the Stones*, exhibition catalogue, Diriyah Contemporary Art Biennale, December 2022.
7 Interviews with Rebecca Anne Proctor, 27 October 2022.
8 Ohoud Al-Najran, interview with Rebecca Anne Proctor, October 2022.
9 'Ministry of Culture, Saudi Art Council launch first summer edition of 21,39', *Saudi Gazette*, 8 June 2019, https://saudigazette.com.sa/article/568349.
10 Mohammed Hafiz, interview with Rebecca Anne Proctor, 27 October 2022.
11 Aarnout Helb, interview with Rebecca Anne Proctor, 11 October 2022.
12 Mohammed Al Faraj, interview with Rebecca Anne Proctor, October 2022.
13 Antonia Carver, interview with Rebecca Anne Proctor, October 2022.
14 Ministry of Culture, Royal Commission for AlUla and the Royal Commission for Riyadh City, among others.
15 Mohammed Hafiz, interview with Rebecca Anne Proctor, 25 October 2022.
16 Stephen Stapleton, interview with Rebecca Anne Proctor, October 2022.
17 Neama Al-Sudairi, interview with Rebecca Anne Proctor, October 2022.
18 Maha Al-Senan, interview with Rebecca Anne Proctor, October 2022.
19 *Feeling the Stones*, op.cit.
20 Kristin Smith Diwan, interview with Rebecca Anne Proctor, 14 October 2022.
21 Email correspondence with Meagan Kelly Horsman, Managing Director, Christie's Middle East, 24 October 2022.
22 Mo Ali, interview with Rebecca Anne Proctor, October 2022.
23 Conversation between Mono Gallery Manager, Usman Malik, and Rebecca Anne Proctor, 24 October 2022.
24 Mohammed Hafiz, interview with Rebecca Anne Proctor, 25 October 2022.
25 All quotes, Aarnout Helb, interview with Rebecca Anne Proctor, 11 October 2022.
26 David Barboza, 'In China's New Revolution, Art Greets Capitalism', *The New York*

Times, 4 January 2007, https://www.nytimes.com/2007/01/04/arts/design/04arti.html. It should be noted that Chinese artists did not have as much government support as those in Saudi Arabia do now. The crash was due to private sector speculation.

27 Moath Alofi, interview with Rebecca Anne Proctor, October 2022.

28 Mohammed Al Faraj, interview with Rebecca Anne Proctor, October 2022.

29 Sultan bin Fahad, interview with Rebecca Anne Proctor, October 2022.

30 Mohammed Al Faraj, interview with Rebecca Anne Proctor, October 2022.

6: Engaging with Saudi Arabia's New Arts Playing Field: Opportunities and New Perspectives

1 Kristin Smith Diwan, interview with Rebecca Anne Proctor, October 2022.

2 Neville Wakefield, interview with Rebecca Anne Proctor, October 2022.

3 Hans Ulrich Obrist, interview with Alia Al-Senussi, November 2022.

4 Quoted in Rebecca Anne Proctor, '"We have our own individual voices": Saudi Artists Debate Their Place in the Kingdom as the West Becomes Wary of its Commitment to Progress', *Artnet News*, 12 September 2019, https://news.artnet.com/art-world/saudi-arabia-artists-1646848.

5 Iwona Blazwick, interview with Rebecca Anne Proctor, October 2022.

6 ibid.

7 Quoted in Gareth Harris, 'From Whitechapel to Saudi Arabia: Iwona Blazwick takes up a new post as AlUla Public Art Supremo'. *The Art Newspaper*, 27 June 2022.

8 Neville Wakefield, interview with Rebecca Anne Proctor, October 2022.

Conclusion: Saudi Arabia's New Creative Economy

1 See Rebecca Anne Proctor, '"We have our own individual voices"', op.cit.

2 Mohammed Al Faraj, interview with Rebecca Anne Proctor, October 2022.

3 Hussein Ibish, 'Why the US-Saudi Crisis is so Bad and So Unnecessary', The Arab Gulf States Institute in Washington website, 14 October 2022, https://agsiw.org/why-the-u-s-saudi-crisis-is-so-bad-and-so-unnecessary/.

4 Maha Al-Senan, interview with Rebecca Anne Proctor, October 2022.

Further Reading

Al Resayes, M. *The History of Fine Arts in Saudi Arabia* (in Arabic) (Ministry of Culture and Information, Riyadh, 2010)

Al-Senan, Maha. 'The Worth of Art: The Future of the Art Market in Saudi Arabia', *International Design Journal*, vol.4, no.1 (2014)

Al-Senan, Maha. 'An Insider's View of Saudi and UAE Arts', *Asian Academic Research Journal of Multidisciplinary Studies*, vol.35, no.1 (January 2015)

Al Shroogi, Bashar. *Fast Forward* (Saudi Art Council, Riyadh, 2014)

Danforth, Loring. *Crossing the Kingdom* (University of California Press, Berkeley, 2016)

Foley, Sean. *Changing Saudi Arabia: Art, Culture, and Society in the Kingdom* (Lynne Rienner Publishers, Boulder, Colorado, 2019)

Ghattas, Kim. *Black Wave: Saudi Arabia, Iran and the Forty-Year Rivalry That Unraveled Culture, Religion, and Collective Memory in the Middle East* (Henry Holt & Company, New York, 2020)

Hope, Bradley and Scheck, Justin. *Blood and Hope: Mohammed bin Salman's Ruthless Quest for Global Power* (Hachette Books, New York, 2021)

Hubbard, Ben. *MBS: The Rise to Power of Mohammed bin Salman* (Harper Collins, New York, 2020)

Kepel, Gilles. *Away from Chaos: The Middle East and the Challenge to the West* (Columbia University Press, New York, 2020)

Lacy, Robert. *Inside the Kingdom: Kings, Clerics, Modernists, Terrorists and the Struggle for Saudi Arabia* (Penguin Books, London, 2009)

Stapleton, Stephen, Booth-Clibborn, Edward, Al-Turki, Abdullah and Jameel, Fady (eds). *Edge of Arabia* (Booth-Clibborn Editions, London, 2012)
Wolff, Jane. *The Social Production of Art* (New York University Press, New York, 1993)
Zuhur, Sherifa. *Middle East in Focus: Saudi Arabia* (ABC-CLIO, Santa Barbara, California, 2011)

Podcasts

'The Art Angle Podcast: What Is Saudi Arabia Trying to Do with Contemporary Art? Rebecca Anne Proctor in conversation with Andrew Goldstein', *Artnet News*, 18 February 2020, https://news.artnet.com/multimedia/art-angle-podcast-saudi-arabia-1779780
'How Saudi Artists Are Driving Political Change. Abu Dhabi Art Focus Podcast', Episode 2, hosted by Aimee Dawson and Anna Somers Cocks, *The Art Newspaper*, 10 November 2017, https://www.theartnewspaper.com/2017/11/10/abu-dhabi-focus-podcast-episode-two-how-saudi-artists-are-driving-political-change

Index